Building Academic Literacy

Audrey Fielding
Ruth Schoenbach
Editors

Building Academic Literacy

An Anthology

for Reading Apprenticeship

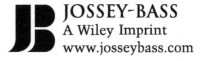

WestEd — Published in Partnership with WestEd

JOSSEY-BASS
A Wiley Imprint
www.josseybass.com

Published by Jossey-Bass
A Wiley Imprint
989 Market Street, San Francisco, CA 94103-1741   www.josseybass.com

Jossey-Bass books and products are available through most bookstores. To contact Jossey-Bass directly call our Customer Care Department within the U.S. at 800-956-7739, outside the U.S. at 317-572-3986, or fax 317-572-4002.

Jossey-Bass also publishes its books in a variety of electronic formats. Some content that appears in print may not be available in electronic books.

Library of Congress Cataloging-in-Publication Data

Building academic literacy : an anthology for reading apprenticeship / Audrey
Fielding, Ruth Schoenbach, editors.—1st ed.
    p. cm. — (Jossey-Bass education series)
Includes bibliographical references.
   ISBN 0-7879-6555-3 (alk. paper)
  1. Reading (Secondary)—United States. 2. Literacy—Social
aspects—United States. I. Fielding, Audrey, 1942— II. Schoenbach,
Ruth. III. Series.
   LB1632 .B76 2003
   428.4'071'2—dc21   2002153517

Printed in the United States of America
FIRST EDITION
PB Printing   15 14 13 12

The Jossey-Bass Education Series

Contents

Part III: How We Read   **159**

Selections describe the different ways our minds work as we
try to understand what we read.

Part IV: Breaking Codes   215

Selections reflect our need to navigate unfamiliar types of texts.

Introduction

"Is anybody in here from Armenia?" a ninth-grade girl asked her classmates. No one answered. She knew the answer was no. "Well, why should we read about it then?"

Classroom conversation moment from an academic literacy class, Thurgood Marshall Academic High School, San Francisco, 1997

Literacy and Identity

Why should we read about other people's lives? Why should we read about places we've never been, have never heard of or cared much about? What's the point of reading? Why do some people hate reading, or feel they are "just not readers," when they are clearly very smart and talented? Why do other people feel that reading helps them survive ?

The selections in Part One of this anthology on the theme of Literacy and Identity provide starting points for your thinking and talking about these kinds of questions. In this first part, you will find a sampling of how others have come to define themselves as readers. Jimmy Santiago Baca's desire to know more about his Latino cultural heritage helps him struggle to understand the words on the page. Richard Wright shares how his discovery of reading came to direct his life.

Literacy and Power

What is the relationship between literacy and power? Societies throughout history and around the world have limited literacy for people as a way to reinforce inequality. Girls in Afghanistan, for example, were not allowed to go to school for many years until the Taliban rule was ended in 2002. Access to a quality education can make a big difference in how much money one is likely to earn throughout a lifetime.

In Part Two of this anthology, Literacy and Power, the selected readings explore these questions and more personal aspects of the relation of literacy to power. We read about the power of reading as it transforms people's lives. Malcolm X finds that reading makes him come "mentally alive." In the poem "Precious Words," Emily Dickinson shares her belief that words can keep our spirits alive in difficult times. Gary Lee, frustrated by his failure to learn how to read in school, realizes years later that he must learn to read and write if he is to function in the world.

How We Read

Imagine yourself, for a moment, reading a cartoon, a menu in a restaurant, an e-mail from friends or family, a favorite magazine or newspaper section, a chapter in a textbook for a science class, or a book your best friend recommended. What exactly goes on in your mind when you are reading these different kinds of texts? Each of us reads differently. We bring our thoughts, experiences, and feelings about ourselves as readers to the words on the page.

Part Three of this anthology explores the questions of how we read. What goes on in our minds as we see the printed words on the page? Eighth-grade student Jennifer Liu offers her advice on how "to create a movie in your head" as you read. In "Superman and Me," Sherman Alexie describes how as a very young boy, he learned to see the world "in paragraphs."

Breaking Codes

The readings in this part present a variety of texts that challenge us because of their specific vocabularies, structures, and purposes. Movies, hip-hop, and science, for example, use coded language, and readers must be able to understand the code. In "Technicality," the author helps us see that scientific terms can be changed from a reading challenge to a key to breaking the codes of scientific concepts. In the humorous essay "Important: Read This First," the seemingly clear directions for reading a book can become a challenge when they are followed exactly as written. And, finally, Herbert Kohl, in "Comic Books," explains the language and structure of comics.

Academic Literacy and the Reading Apprenticeship™ Framework

We created this anthology for students and teachers in "Academic Literacy" classes based on the model described in *Reading for Understanding: A Guide to Improving Reading in Middle and High School Classrooms*, by Ruth Schoenbach, Cynthia Greenleaf, Christine Cziko, and Lori Hurwitz (Jossey-Bass, 1999). We also offer it to students and teachers in other classrooms. The Reading Apprenticeship™ framework described in *Reading for Understanding* can be a powerful guide for building a community of readers. We offer this anthology to support and enrich the conversations in your classroom communities.

Audrey Fielding, Consultant
Ruth Schoenbach, Codirector
Strategic Literacy Initiative
WestEd
300 Lakeside Drive, 18th Floor
Oakland, CA 94612
(510) 302-4255

Part I

Literacy and Identity

Selections describe the different ways people see themselves as readers.

1

"Sharon Cho," from *Speaking of Reading*

Sharon Cho

*Cho's childhood passion for comic books has extended
into her adult life. Like one of her beloved superheroes,
Cho tries to do right by the people she encounters,
including the many comic book artists whose careers
she now manages.*

I grew up in Singapore speaking Chinese at home and English in
school, but English is my primary reading and writing language.
As a young child, I read everything I could get my hands on, especially comic books. My mother says I'm so nearsighted because I
used to read under the bedspread with a flashlight. I was very sick
between the ages of four and twelve and was bedridden a lot. I was
only in school about 30 percent of the time, so reading was my main
form of entertainment.

Reading comic books gave me a sense of being special. I always
wanted to be a superhero, and I still do. I probably had ten to fifteen stacks of comic books about two feet high each. Most of them
were hand-me-downs from a friend who gave them to my sister first,
who then handed them down to me. The others I bought myself.
Comic books opened up my imagination and gave me a large vocabulary, too. What other six-year-old would know what a serum was?
Or invulnerability? Or radar? I picked up so many things in comic
books having to do with super powers and stuff like that. As a result,

my English became a lot better. My mother didn't care what I read, as long as I kept out of trouble, but she did finally make a rule that I couldn't bring comic books to the dinner table.

I'm one of the few females I know who grew up on superheroes and really took them to heart. Only a few of the superheroes were women, and it was very hard to find them. There was Supergirl and Batgirl, and later there was Miss Marvel and Spiderwoman and a few others that aren't worth mentioning. I wanted to be Supergirl. She was the innocent one, the pure of heart, the one that never questioned what she did, she just did it. She was a teenager, and for a few years we were the same age. About ten years ago, she died and I sobbed. Now there's a new Supergirl, but I can't stand the new one.

Comics instilled in me a very profound sense of "truth, justice, and the American way." Ha, ha. They gave me the belief that one person *can* make a difference. There's one phrase that came out of *Spiderman:* "With great power comes great responsibility." And Superman would never, never stoop to the level of the villains. He was above that. There was always a real difference between a good guy and a bad guy in the old comic books. Good guys always found a way to defeat the bad guys, and used honorable methods to do it.

I really don't like the ways heroes are portrayed in comic books these days. There's no longer any clear line between heroes and villains. Heroes kill people and don't care. Today's superheroes still believe in what they do, but they don't question—they just go ahead and kill. That really sickens me. But some of the new comic books are adult oriented and have darker themes, which I do like. Those heroes are very confused most of the time, which is more like reality.

Comic books are like American myths. I also loved the Greek myths—reading about Hercules is like reading a comic book—here is another hero who is able to do super fantastic things, but still has human failings. I loved the Greek myths, but not the Roman myths. I always felt the Romans were cheap rip-offs. In fact, whenever I hear somebody calling a god or goddess by his or her Roman name,

I still get angry. Artemis is *not* Diana. Diana is a watered-down version of Artemis. Artemis and Apollo were my two favorites—Apollo because he was god of the light and Artemis, who was his twin sister, was the goddess of the Moon. Of all the other Greek goddesses, Athena was too cold, Aphrodite was too lusty, and Hera was too jealous. Artemis was just the strong, silent one, the one with passion. She was more of a superhero.

I had a huge set of Bible stories that my aunt sent from the States. I absorbed those Bible stories in the same way I absorbed comic books and Greek myths. I saw Christ as a superior. He died for the good of mankind. He was so good that nobody could understand him. He was perfect. He was the son of God. The prophets were much the same. I see Mohammed and Buddha in the same light also, because they achieved enlightenment. Yes, there are definite parallels between the Bible stories and the superhero comic books that I read.

Reading about superheroes gave me delusions of grandeur. I'd like to think I am grand, but I have many friends who would tell you I've done stupid things thinking I was a superhero. For example, I chased down four men into a tough section of town because they sideswiped my car. I didn't care what happened to me; what I cared about was that they apologize, that they do something about my car, that justice be carried out.

When I turned thirty last year, I made a promise to myself that I was going to try and make sure that every action I did was something admirable. I still want to be a superhero and I'm very, very tough on myself. I can't stand it when I feel I'm using or manipulating people, or anything that I feel isn't heroic in some sense of the word. I've tried to take what I read and put it into my life in some way. I'm an idealist in my heart and believe that somehow if people listened more and took the experiences around them more to heart, maybe the world would be a nicer place.

My family doesn't understand that my value system comes from superheroes. It tears my heart out when I see homeless people on the street and I've befriended a few of them. I wish I could do more. My family sees that as the irresponsible part of me. They see me give away my money. One of the conditions of my family helping me to buy my condo is that I'm not allowed to shelter anyone. They see it as foolishness when I take people in and give them a place to stay.

I don't know who I would be if I hadn't read comic books as a kid. Comic books influenced me to be a good person, a hero in my own way.

2

"Kevin Clarke," from Speaking of Reading

Kevin Clarke

*Clarke, a high school sophomore, is frustrated by
his inability to concentrate while reading novels and
textbooks, and admits it is finally time for him to
come to grips with his reading difficulties.*

My fourth-grade teacher was really horrible. She called me stupid when I didn't understand something. She'd just scream at me when I asked questions and make me feel like I was the stupidest person on earth. I wanted to learn the stuff, too. That was back when it wasn't cool to be the screw-off in class like it was in seventh grade. It was sheer frustration. My parents wanted me to read, but I just wasn't doing it. I wasn't passing any of the tests either, only cheating on them. I didn't understand the reading and I didn't like it. I had the feeling of being the supremely dumbest kid around. All the other kids seemed to be able to read. There was one girl in my class who was reading *Gone with the Wind*. I hate her still.

When I was in fifth grade I read a book called *The Lemon Meringue Dog*. It was the only book I ever enjoyed reading. My mother even took a picture of me reading it which is still tacked to the kitchen cabinet. My parents made me read it. They said, "You have to read something for fun, damn it. If you don't read something for fun, we're going to ground you." So I read it for fun and actually enjoyed it. Then they suggested I should read another one, but I couldn't. I was too afraid I wouldn't be able to understand another book. The fact that I understood that one was a mystery to me.

I went to a small island in Maine with my friend and his parents during the summer between eighth and ninth grade. We'd go boating and take short swims in the freezing water, and just kick around. I felt kind of uncomfortable because all three of them were reading a lot of the time and I'd be doing something else like walking around the island or something. The only books they had were some really old ones and a few supermarket novels. My friend started reading a book about some insurance fraud thing. It was OK for him, but the print was too fine for me to read. I think they were uncomfortable that I wasn't reading. Maybe they thought I was stupid or something, so they said, "How about a book?" I froze up but I said, "OK." They found a book for me called *Wifey*, by Judy Blume, but written for adults. They read some of the explicit pages to me and that got my teenage self interested. It was about this housewife who had this asshole of a husband, really not a cool guy, you know? He wouldn't even let her mourn the death of Kennedy because he voted for the other guy. I liked the story, but when it got into what she was thinking and all that, I just couldn't understand it, so I quit. Reading is a waste of time for me unless I understand the book, which is rare.

I guess people who read all the time must get something out of it that I just haven't experienced. They must take in the material and really understand it. I don't know whether they force themselves to read or not. I'm sure there are a lot of people who don't want to read, but at least they can if they have to. I think good readers must be interested in whatever they're reading about, or they must find interesting things in a book after they start reading. They must, how else could they read if they weren't interested? I know I can't. If I'm not interested in a book it becomes completely boring; it's just impossible for me to keep reading.

I recently read some of *Brave New World*, but only after it was assigned to us a second time. The first time I didn't read any of it; I didn't like it, I was not turned on to it. I didn't understand the first page. One character would be talking and then someone else would be talking—it was too complicated. I thought it was the same person and I got confused and angry. Why were they making me read this? It didn't make any sense to me, but it did make sense to some of the other guys.

I don't hear the voices of the characters in books, but I do try to envision what I'm reading. When I was reading *Brave New World*, I pictured the main character as this guy I know who is thin and wiry and wears glasses. I always relate characters to people I've seen before because I can't make up somebody I've never seen. Places are hard to imagine, too. I have to borrow a place I've already seen.

I saw this movie that was a play of *A Tale of Two Cities*. We read the book beforehand in class, and I bought the Cliff Notes. But when I saw the movie, the people and scenes were much different than I had envisioned them. There was one character, a woman who I expected to be old, feeble, and crotched over, but in the movie she wasn't like this at all. I assumed I was wrong and the movie was right, because the people who made the movie are smarter than I am and so they understood the book better. I don't trust myself to read it right.

When I got into the eighth, ninth, and tenth grades, reading became a really difficult process because I had to read a lot for school. Each night I might have to read fifteen pages in a biology book, ten pages in an English book, and fifteen more for history. That's an immense amount for me. I start to read, and I get down the first line, OK, second line, OK, third line, OK, but I just can't concentrate after that. I'm reading but my mind is trying to distract me from the book. It's the most frustrating feeling. I say, "OK, think," and slap myself on the face, and go back to the beginning. Or I ask myself, "What have I just read?" and I know nothing about what I just read. I might have read six pages and I know nothing.

I get totally uncomfortable when I try to read, and there are always other things I'd rather be doing than making myself uncomfortable and straining myself. I get embarrassed when I read, not because there's someone else around, but because I embarrass myself when I can't do it. I say, "Jeez, you're fifteen and you can't read a whole book, or even a chapter." Why should I put myself in this kind of discomfort on purpose? Sure, I have to do school work, but I can call up a friend to brief me on the chapter, or if I have to answer questions from the reading, I can skim, looking for the important words and write out the answers. I'm definitely smart in a lot of other subjects, but when it gets down to reading, there I am, in the thirteenth percentile.

I've known about my reading problem for a while now, and I'm starting to hit hard on it. I realize it's not something I can just work more on and have it go away. I really have to come out of the closet with my reading problem.

3

"Inside Out," from *The Circuit: Stories from the Life of a Migrant Child*

Francisco Jiménez

In his autobiography, The Circuit, *Jiménez, the son of migrant farmworkers, shares his story of going to school for the first time. Unable to understand English, he sits in the classroom and watches a caterpillar in a jar on a wooden counter near his desk. As time goes by and the caterpillar changes into a butterfly, Jiménez experiences his own development.*

I remember being hit on the wrists with a twelve-inch ruler because I did not follow directions in class," Roberto answered in a mildly angry tone when I asked him about his first year of school. "But how could I?" he continued, "the teacher gave them in English."

"So what did you do?" I asked, rubbing my wrists.

"I always guessed what the teacher wanted me to do. And when she did not use the ruler on me, I knew I had guessed right," he responded. "Some of the kids made fun of me when I tried to say something in English and got it wrong," he went on. "I had to repeat first grade."

I wish I had not asked him, but he was the only one in the family, including Papá and Mamá, who had attended school. I walked away. I did not speak or understand English either, and I already felt anxious. Besides, I was excited about going to school for the first time that following Monday. It was late January and we had just returned, a week before, from Corcoran where my family picked cotton. We settled in "Tent City," a labor camp owned by Sheehey Strawberry Farms located about ten miles east of Santa Maria.

On our first day of school, Roberto and I got up early. I dressed in a pair of overalls, which I hated because they had suspenders, and a flannel checkered shirt, which Mamá had bought at the Goodwill store. As I put on my cap, Roberto reminded me that it was bad manners to wear a hat indoors. I thought of leaving it at home so that I would not make the mistake of forgetting to take it off in class, but I decided to wear it. Papá always wore a cap and I did not feel completely dressed for school without it.

On our way out to catch the school bus, Roberto and I said goodbye to Mamá. Papá had already left to look for work, either topping carrots or thinning lettuce. Mamá stayed home to take care of Trampita, and to rest because she was expecting another baby.

When the school bus arrived, Roberto and I climbed in and sat together. I took the window seat and, on the way, watched endless rows of lettuce and cauliflower whiz by. The furrows that came up to the two lane road looked like giant legs running alongside us. The bus made several stops to pick up kids and, with each stop, the noise inside got louder. Some kids were yelling at the top of their lungs. I did not know what they were saying. I was getting a headache. Roberto had his eyes closed and was frowning. I did not disturb him. I figured he was getting a headache too.

By the time we got to Main Street School, the bus was packed. The bus driver parked in front of the red brick building and opened the door. We all poured out. Roberto, who had attended the school the year before, accompanied me to the main office where we met the principal, Mr. Sims, a tall, red-headed man with bushy eyebrows and hairy hands. He patiently listened to Roberto who, using the little English he knew, managed to enroll me in the first grade.

Mr. Sims walked me to my classroom. I liked it as soon as I saw it because, unlike our tent, it had wooden floors, electric lights, and heat. It felt cozy. He introduced me to my teacher, Miss Scalapino, who smiled, repeating my name, "Francisco." It was the only word I understood the whole time she and the principal talked. They repeated it each time they glanced at me. After he left, she showed me to my desk, which was at the end of the row of desks closest to the windows. There were no other kids in the room yet.

I sat at my desk and ran my hand over its wooden top. It was full of scratches and dark, almost black, ink spots. I opened the top and inside were a book, a box of crayons, a yellow ruler, a thick pencil, a pair of scissors. To my left, under the windows, was a dark wooden counter the length of the room. On top of it, right next to my desk, was a caterpillar in a large jar. It looked just like the ones I had seen in the fields. It was yellowish green with black bands and it moved very slowly without making any sound.

I was about to put my hand in the jar to touch the caterpillar when the bell rang. All the kids lined up outside the classroom door and then walked in quietly and took their seats. Some of them looked at me and giggled. Embarrassed and nervous, I looked at the caterpillar in the jar. I did this every time someone looked at me.

Miss Scalapino started speaking to the class and I did not understand a word she was saying. The more she spoke, the more anxious I became. By the end of the day, I was very tired of hearing Miss Scalapino talk because the sounds made no sense to me. I thought that perhaps by paying close attention, I would begin to understand, but I did not. I only got a headache, and that night, when I went to bed, I heard her voice in my head.

For days I got headaches from trying to listen, until I learned a way out. When my head began to hurt, I let my mind wander. Sometimes I imagined myself flying out of the classroom and over the fields where Papá worked and landing next to him and surprising him. But when I daydreamed, I continued to look at the teacher and pretend I was paying attention because Papá told me it was disrespectful not to pay attention, especially to grown-ups.

It was easier when Miss Scalapino read to the class from a book with illustrations because I made up my own stories, in Spanish, based on the pictures. She held the book with both hands above her head and walked around the classroom to make sure everyone got a chance to see the pictures, most of which were of animals. I enjoyed looking at them and making up stories, but I wished I understood what she was reading.

In time I learned some of my classmates' names. The one I heard the most and therefore learned first was "Curtis." Curtis was the biggest, strongest, and most popular kid in the class. Everyone wanted to be his friend and to play with him. He was always chosen captain when the kids formed teams. Since I was the smallest kid in the class and did not know English, I was chosen last.

I preferred to hang around Arthur, one of the boys who knew a little Spanish. During recess, he and I played on the swings and I pretended to be a Mexican movie star, like Jorge Negrete or Pedro Infante, riding a horse and singing the *corridos* we often heard on the car radio. I sang them to Arthur as we swung back and forth, going as high as we could.

But when I spoke to Arthur in Spanish and Miss Scalapino heard me, she said "NO!" with body and soul. Her head turned left and right a hundred times a second and her index finger moved from side to side as fast as a windshield wiper on a rainy day. "English, English," she repeated. Arthur avoided me whenever she was around.

Often during recess I stayed with the caterpillar. Sometimes it was hard to spot him because he blended in with the green leaves and twigs. Every day I brought him leaves from the pepper and cypress tress that grew on the playground.

Just in front of the caterpillar, lying on top of the cabinet, was a picture book of caterpillars and butterflies. I went through it, page by page, studying all the pictures and running my fingers lightly over the caterpillars and the bright wings of the butterflies and the many patterns on them. I knew caterpillars turned into butterflies because Roberto had told me, but I wanted to know more. I was sure information was in the words written underneath each picture in large black letters. I tried to figure them out by looking at the pictures. I did this so many times that I could close my eyes and see the words, but I could not understand what they meant.

My favorite time in school was when we did art, which was every afternoon, after the teacher had read to us. Since I did not understand Miss Scalapino when she explained the art lessons, she let me do whatever I wanted. I drew all kinds of animals but mostly birds and butterflies. I sketched them in pencil and then colored them using every color in my crayon box. Miss Scalapino even tacked one of my drawings up on the board for everyone to see. After a couple of weeks it disappeared and I did not know how to ask where it had gone.

One cold Thursday morning, during recess, I was the only kid on the playground without a jacket. Mr. Sims must have noticed I was shivering because that afternoon, after school, he took me to his office and pulled out a green jacket from a large cardboard box that was full of used clothes and toys. He handed it to me and gestured for me to try it on. It smelled like graham crackers. I put it on, but it was too big, so he rolled up the sleeves about two inches to make it fit. I took it home and showed it off to my parents. They smiled. I liked it because it was green and it hid my suspenders.

The next day I was on the playground wearing my new jacket and waiting for the first bell to ring when I saw Curtis coming at me like an angry bull. Aiming his head directly at me, and pulling his arms straight back with his hands clenched, he stomped up to me and started yelling. I did not understand him, but I knew it had something to do with the jacket because he began to pull on it, trying to take it off me. Next thing I knew he and I were on the ground wrestling. Kids circled around us. I could hear them yelling Curtis's name and something else. I knew I had no chance, but I stubbornly held on to my jacket. He pulled on one of the sleeves so hard that it ripped at the shoulder. He pulled on the right pocket and it ripped. Then Miss Scalapino's face appeared above. She pushed Curtis off of me and grabbed me by the back of the collar and picked me up off the ground. It took all the power I had not to cry.

On the way to the classroom Arthur told me that Curtis claimed the jacket was his, that he had lost it at the beginning of the year. He also said that the teacher told Curtis and me that we were being punished. We had to sit on the bench during recess for the rest of the week. I did not see the jacket again. Curtis got it but I never saw him wear it.

For the rest of the day, I could not even pretend I was paying attention to Miss Scalapino, I was so embarrassed. I laid my head on top of my desk and closed my eyes. I kept thinking about what had happened that morning. I wanted to fall asleep and wake up to find it was only a dream. The teacher called my name but I did not answer. I heard her walk up to me. I did not know what to expect. She gently shook me by the shoulders. Again, I did not respond. Miss Scalapino must have thought I was asleep because she left me alone, even when it was time for recess and everyone left the room.

Once the room was quiet, I slowly opened my eyes. I had had them closed for so long that the sunlight coming through the windows blinded me. I rubbed my eyes with the back of my hands and then looked to my left at the jar. I looked for the caterpillar but could not see it. Thinking it might be hidden, I put my hand in the jar and lightly stirred the leaves. To my surprise, the caterpillar had spun itself into a cocoon and had attached itself to a small twig. It looked like a tiny, cotton bulb, just like Roberto had said it would. I gently stroked it with my index finger, picturing it asleep and peaceful.

At the end of the school day, Miss Scalapino gave me a note to take home to my parents. Papá and Mamá did not know how to read, but they did not have to. As soon as they saw my swollen upper lip and the scratches on my left cheek, they knew what the note said. When I told them what happened, they were very upset but relieved that I did not disrespect the teacher.

For the next several days, going to school and facing Miss Scalapino was harder than ever. However, I slowly began to get over what happened that Friday. Once I got used to the routine in school and I picked up some English words, I felt more comfortable in class.

On Wednesday, May 23, a few days before the end of the school year, Miss Scalapino took me by surprise. After we were all sitting down and she had taken roll, she called for everyone's attention. I did not understand what she said, but I heard her say my name as she held up a blue ribbon. She then picked up my drawing of the butterfly that had disappeared weeks before and held it up for everyone to see. She walked up to me and handed me the drawing and the silk blue ribbon that had a number one printed on it in gold. I knew then I had received first prize for my drawing. I was so proud I felt like bursting out of my skin. My classmates, including Curtis, stretched their necks to see the ribbon.

That afternoon, during our free period, I went over to check on the caterpillar. I turned the jar around, trying to see the cocoon. It was beginning to crack open. I excitedly cried out, "Look, look," pointing to it. The whole class, like a swarm of bees, rushed over to the counter. Miss Scalapino took the jar and placed it on top of a desk in the middle of the classroom so everyone could see it. For the next several minutes we all stood here watching the butterfly emerge from its cocoon, in slow motion.

At the end of the day, just before the last bell, Miss Scalapino picked up the jar and took the class outside to the playground. She placed the jar on the ground and we all circled around her. I had a hard time seeing over the other kids so, Miss Scalapino called me, and motioned for me to open the jar. I broke through the circle, knelt on the ground, and unscrewed the top. Like magic, the butterfly flew into the air, fluttering its wings up and down.

After school I waited in line for my bus in front of the playground. I proudly carried the blue ribbon in my right hand and the drawing in the other. Arthur and Curtis came up and stood behind me to wait for their bus. Curtis motioned for me to show him the drawing again. I held it up so he could see it.

"He really likes it, Francisco," Arthur said to me in Spanish.

"*¿Cómo se dice 'es tuyo' in inglés?*" I asked.

"It's yours," answered Arthur.

"It's yours," I repeated handing the drawing to Curtis.

4

From *The Acts of King Arthur and His Noble Knights*

John Steinbeck

*Steinbeck tells that us that books for him "were
printed demons—the tongs and thumbscrews of
outrageous persecution." He recalls the agony of
learning how to read. But one day, an aunt gives him
a copy of* King Arthur, *and the magic begins. The
language of Old English seduces him into the mystery
and adventure of medieval times.*

Some people there are who, being grown, forget the horrible task
of learning to read. It is perhaps the greatest single effort that
the human undertakes, and he must do it as a child. An adult is
rarely successful in the undertaking—the reduction of experience
to a set of symbols. For a thousand thousand years these humans
have existed and they have only learned this trick—this magic—in
the final ten thousand of the thousand thousand.

I do not know how usual my experience is, but I have seen in
my children the appalled agony of trying to learn to read. They, at
least, have my experience.

I remember that words—written or printed—were devils, and
books, because they gave me pain, were my enemies.

Some literature was in the air around me. The Bible I absorbed
through my skin. My uncles exuded Shakespeare, and *Pilgrim's
Progress* was mixed with my mother's milk. But these things came

into my ears. They were sounds, rhythms, figures. Books were printed demons—the tongs and thumbscrews of outrageous persecution. And then, one day, an aunt gave me a book and fatuously ignored my resentment. I stared at the black print with hatred, and then, gradually, the pages opened and let me in. The magic happened. The Bible and Shakespeare and *Pilgrim's Progress* belonged to everyone. But this was mine—It was a cut version of the Caxton *Morte d'Arthur* of Thomas Malory. I loved the old spelling of the words—and the words no longer used. Perhaps a passionate love for the English language opened to me from this one book. I was delighted to find out paradoxes—that *cleave* means both to stick together and to cut apart; that *host* means both an enemy and a welcoming friend; that *king* and *gens* (people) stem from the same root. For a long time, I had a secret language—*yclept* and *hyght, wist*—and *accord* meaning peace, and *entente* meaning purpose, and *fyaunce* meaning promise. Moving my lips, I pronounced the letter known as *thorn*, þ, like a "p," which it resembles, instead of like a "th." But in my town, the first word of Ye Old Pye Shoppe was pronounced "yee," so I guess my betters were no better off than I. It was much later that I discovered the "y" had been substituted for the lost þ. But beyond the glorious and secret words—"And when the chylde is borne lete it be delyvered to me at yonder privy posterne uncrystened"—oddly enough I knew the words from whispering them to myself. The very strangeness of the language dyd me enchante, and vaulted me into an ancient scene.

And in that scene were all the vices that ever were—and courage and sadness and frustration, but particularly gallantry—perhaps the only single quality of man that the West has invented. I think my sense of right and wrong, my feeling of noblesse oblige, and any thought I may have against the oppressor and for the oppressed, came from this secret book. It did not outrage my sensibilities as nearly all the children's books did. It did not seem strange to me that Uther Pendragon wanted the wife of his vassal and took her by trickery. I was not frightened to find that there were evil knights, as well as noble ones. In my own town there were men who wore the clothes of virtue whom I knew to be bad. In pain or sorrow or confusion, I went back to my magic book. Children are violent and cruel—and good—and I was all of these—and all of these were in the secret book. If I could not choose my way at the crossroads of love and loyalty, neither could Lancelot. I could understand the darkness of Mordred because he was in me too; and there was some Galahad in me, but perhaps not enough. The Grail feeling was there, however, deep-planted, and perhaps always will be.

"My Back Pages," from *The Most Wonderful Books: Writers on Discovering the Pleasures of Reading*

Greg Sarris

Sarris, a writer from Santa Rosa, California, shares the joy he derived from listening to stories told around the dinner table, on porches, and in front of the grocery store. A poor high school student in remedial classes, he decides to work hard on reading, thinking that it may make him rich. It isn't until college that he begins to enjoy reading.

I was never a *natural* reader, if there is such a thing. As a kid, I didn't go to libraries. I didn't read late into the night, hiding under the covers with a flashlight devouring adventure stories, comics, or Boy Scout manuals. Aside from vague memories of *Dick and Jane*, which I had to read in school, I can't think of anything I read until my freshman year in high school when I was forced to read *The Old Man and the Sea* in my remedial English class. I felt sorry for the fish.

At the time, when I was about fifteen, I was still a street kid, living with American Indian families and others in and around South Park, a poor section of Santa Rosa, California, where the "minorities" lived, the Blacks, Mexicans, Indians, poor Anglos. I am mixed, American Indian (Kashaya Pomo/Coast Miwok) and Filipino on my father's side, Jewish and German on my mother's.

What I knew best were the stories people *told*. On front porches, at the dinner table, in front of the corner grocery, I *listened* to stories.

. . . Stories about Old Uncle, an Indian doctor, how he once took a woodpecker's bones out of Grandma's eyes, how he could turn into a hummingbird and make it from our front porch to the Old Courthouse Square uptown fast as you could blink an eye; stories about Crazy Ida, a black woman who sold smack until she fell in love with Delfino, the Filipino farmworker who played harmonica each Sunday morning in front of the corner grocery; stories about Manuel and Robert, the Portuguese guys who taught me how to box, about the fights, their women, their run-ins with the law. Stories, stories, stories, stories. . . . And I was a pretty good storyteller, too. With wide eyes and a way with words, embellishment and flair, I told others the stories I had heard as well as those I had just plain made up. "You're going to come back in the next life a gossipy old Indian woman," a friend once told me.

I started reading seriously during my junior year in high school, not because I wanted to. I was forced to. I wanted to get rich, the Horatio Alger thing, so I began studying, pulling myself out of remedial classes. In a college prep English class I read short stories by Hemingway, Steinbeck, Fitzgerald. I particularly remember Faulkner's "A Rose for Emily," and it would be Faulkner's stories (and eventually his novels) that made the most sense to me, that seemed most familiar—Yoknapatawpha County with its myriad storytellers, those folks on front porches telling tales about themselves and one another, endlessly.

Eventually when I began to enjoy reading (and finally changed my major in college to English), I knew why. I had been lonesome. Studying night after night alone in my room, I was separated from the life I knew, the voices of people talking in Santa Rosa, the stories. Reading filled the void. Good books became for me good gossip. I read to hear people talking about one another. And it's no wonder that to this day I like best those books about particular communities, those novels, large and small, filled with different characters, different voices crisscrossing in one place.

6

"Seis," from *Bless Me, Ultima*

Rudolfo A. Anaya

This selection tells the story of Antonio's first day at school. He does not speak English. His grandmother, Ultima, says he will be a scholar someday. His friend Jasón tells him to copy the letters that he will see in school. They are magic to Anthony, and he learns to write his name. Yet he will never forget the loneliness of being an outsider.

On the first day of school I awoke with a sick feeling in my stomach. It did not hurt, it just made me feel weak. The sun did not sing as it came over the hill. Today I would take the goat path and trek into town for years and years of schooling. For the first time I would be away from the protection of my mother. I was excited and sad about it.

I heard my mother enter her kitchen, her realm in the castle the giants had built. I heard her make the fire grow and sing with the kindling she fed to it.

Then I heard my father groan. "¡Ay Dios, otro día! Another day and more miles of that cursed highway to patch! And for whom? For me that I might travel west! Ay no, that highway is not for the poor man, it is for the tourist—ay, María, we should have gone to California when we were young, when my sons were boys—"

He was sad. The breakfast dishes rattled.

"Today is Antonio's first day at school," she said.

"Huh! Another expense. In California, they say, the land flows with milk and honey—"

"Any land will flow with milk and honey if it is worked with honest hands!" my mother retorted. "Look at what my brothers have done with the bottomland of El Puerto—"

"Ay, *mujer*, always your brothers! On this hill only rocks grow!"

"Ay! And whose fault is it that we bought a worthless hill! No, you couldn't buy fertile land along the river, you had to buy this piece of, of—"

"Of the llano," my father finished.

"Yes!"

"It is beautiful," he said with satisfaction.

"It is worthless! Look how hard we worked on the garden all summer, and for what? Two baskets of chile and one of corn! Bah!"

"There is freedom here."

"Try putting that in the lunch pails of your children!"

"Tony goes to school today, huh?" he said.

"Yes. And you must talk to him."

"He will be all right."

"He must know the value of his education," she insisted. "He must know what he can become."

"A priest."

"Yes."

"For your brothers." His voice was cold.

"You leave my brothers out of this! They are honorable men. They have always treated you with respect. They were the first colonizers of the Llano Estacado. It was the Lunas who carried the charter from the Mexican government to settle the valley. That took courage—"

"Led by the priest," my father interrupted. I listened intently. I did not yet know the full story of the first Luna priest.

"What? What did you say? Do not dare to mention blasphemy where the children can hear, Gabriel Márez!" She scolded him and chased him out of the kitchen. "Go feed the animals! Give Tony a few minutes extra sleep!" I heard him laugh as he went out.

"My poor baby," she whispered, and then I heard her praying. I heard Deborah and Theresa getting up. They were excited about school because they had already been there. They dressed and ran downstairs to wash.

I heard Ultima enter the kitchen. She said good morning to my mother and turned to help prepare breakfast. Her sound in the kitchen gave me the courage I needed to leap out of bed and into the freshly pressed clothes my mother had readied for me. The new shoes felt strange to feet that had run bare for almost seven years.

"Ay! My man of learning!" my mother smiled when I entered the kitchen. She swept me in her arms and before I knew it she was crying on my shoulder. "My baby will be gone today," she sobbed.

"He will be all right," Ultima said. "The sons must leave the sides of their mothers," she said almost sternly and pulled my mother gently.

"Yes, Grande," my mother nodded, "it's just that he is so small— the last one to leave me—" I thought she would cry all over again. "Go and wash, and comb," she said simply.

I scrubbed my face until it was red. I wet my black hair and combed it. I looked at my dark face in the mirror.

Jasón had said there were secrets in the letters. What did he mean?

"Antoniooooo! Come and eat."

"Tony goes to school, Tony goes to school!" Theresa cried.

"Hush! He shall be a scholar," my mother smiled and served me first. I tried to eat but the food stuck to the roof of my mouth.

"Remember you are a Luna—"

"And a Márez," my father interrupted her. He came in from feeding the animals.

Deborah and Theresa sat aside and divided the school supplies they had bought in town the day before. Each got a Red Chief tablet, crayons, and pencils. I got nothing. "We are ready, mamá!" they cried.

Jasón had said look at the letter carefully, draw it on the tablet, or on the sand of the playground. You will see, it has magic.

"You are to bring honor to your family," my mother cautioned. "Do nothing that will bring disrespect on our good name."

I looked at Ultima. Her magic. The magic of Jasón's Indian. They could not save me now.

"Go immediately to Miss Maestas. Tell her you are my boy. She knows my family. Hasn't she taught them all? Deborah, take him to Miss Maestas."

"Gosh, okay, let's go!"

"Ay! What good does an education do them," my father filled his coffee cup, "they only learn to speak like Indians. Gosh, okay, what kind of words are those?"

"An education will make him a scholar, like—like the old Luna priest."

"A scholar already, on his first day of school!"

"Yes!" my mother retorted. "You know the signs at his birth were good. You remember, Grande, you offered him all the objects of life when he was just a baby, and what did he choose, the pen and the paper—"

"True," Ultima agreed.

"¡Bueno! ¡Bueno!" my father gave in to them. "If that is what he is to be then it is so. A man cannot struggle against his own fate. In my own day we were given no schooling. Only the ricos could afford school. Me, my father gave me a saddle blanket and a wild pony when I was ten. There is your life, he said, and he pointed to the llano. So the llano was my school, it was my teacher, it was my first love—"

"It is time to go, mamá," Deborah interrupted.

"Ay, but those were beautiful years," my father continued. "The llano was still virgin, there was grass as high as the stirrups of a grown horse, there was rain—and then the *tejano* came and built his fences, the railroad came, the roads—it was like a bad wave of the ocean covering all that was good—"

"Yes, it is time, Gabriel," my mother said, and I noticed she touched him gently.

"Yes," my father answered, "so it is. Be respectful to your teachers," he said to us. "And you, Antonio," he smiled, "*suerte.*" It made me feel good. Like a man.

"Wait!" My mother held Deborah and Theresa back, "we must have a blessing. Grande, please bless my children." She made us kneel with her in front of Ultima. "And especially bless my Antonio, that all may go well for him and that he may be a man of great learning—"

Even my father knelt for the blessing. Huddled in the kitchen we bowed our heads. There was no sound.

"*En el nombre del Padre, del Hijo, y el Espíritu Santo—*"

I felt Ultima's hand on my head and at the same time I felt a great force, like a whirlwind, swirl about me. I looked up in fright, thinking the wind would knock me off my knees. Ultima's bright eyes held me still.

In the summer the dust devils of the llano are numerous. They come from nowhere, made by the heat of hell they carry with them the evil spirit of a devil, they lift sand and papers in their path. It is bad luck to let one of these small whirlwinds strike you. But it is easy to ward off the dust devil, it is easy to make it change its path and skirt around you. The power of God is so great. All you have to do is to lift up your right hand and cross your right thumb over your first finger in the form of the cross. No evil can challenge that cross, and the swirling dust with the devil inside must turn away from you.

Once I did not make the sign of the cross on purpose. I challenged the wind to strike me. The twister struck with such force that it knocked me off my feet and left me trembling on the ground. I had never felt such fear before, because as the whirlwind blew its debris around me the gushing wind seemed to call my name:

Antoniooooooooooooooo . . .

Then it was gone, and its evil was left imprinted on my soul.

"¡Antonio!"

"What?"

"Do you feel well? Are you all right?" It was my mother speaking.

But how could the blessing of Ultima be like the whirlwind? Was the power of good and evil the same?

"You may stand up now." My mother helped me to my feet. Deborah and Theresa were already out the door. The blessing was done. I stumbled to my feet, picked up my sack lunch, and started towards the door.

"Tell me, Grande, please," my mother begged.

"María!" my father said sternly.

"Oh, please tell me what my son will be," my mother glanced anxiously from me to Ultima.

"He will be a man of learning," Ultima said sadly.

"¡Madre de Dios!" my mother cried and crossed herself. She turned to me and shouted, "Go! Go!"

I looked at the three of them standing there, and I felt that I was seeing them for the last time: Ultima in her wisdom, my mother in her dream, and my father in his rebellion.

"¡Adios!" I cried and ran out. I followed the two she-goats hopping up the path ahead of me. They sang and I brayed into the morning air, and the pebbles of the path rang as we raced with time towards the bridge. Behind me I heard my mother cry my name.

At the big juniper tree where the hill sloped to the bridge I heard Ultima's owl sing. I knew it was her owl because it was singing in daylight. High at the top by a clump of the ripe blue berries of the juniper I saw it. Its bright eyes looked down on me and it cried, whoooo, whoooo. I took confidence from its song, and wiping the tears from my eyes I raced towards the bridge, the link to town.

I was almost halfway across the bridge when someone called "Race!" I turned and saw a small, thin figure start racing towards me from the far end of the bridge. I recognized the Vitamin Kid.

Race? He was crazy! I was almost half way across. "Race!" I called, and ran. I found out that morning that no one had ever beaten the Vitamin Kid across the bridge, his bridge. I was a good runner and I ran as hard as I could, but just before I reached the other side the clatter of hoofbeats passed me by, the Kid smiled a "Hi Tony," and snorting and leaving a trail of saliva threads in the air, he was gone.

No one knew the Vitamin Kid's real name, no one knew where he lived. He seemed older than the rest of the kids he went to school with. He never stopped long enough to talk, he was always on the run, a blur of speed.

I walked slowly after I crossed the bridge, partly because I was tired and partly because of the dread of school. I walked past Rosie's house, turned, and passed in front of the Longhorn Saloon. When I got to Main Street I was astounded. It seemed as if a million kids were shoutinggruntingpushingcrying their way to school. For a long time I was held hypnotized by the thundering herd, then with a cry of resolution exploding from my throat I rushed into the melee.

Somehow I got to the schoolgrounds, but I was lost. The school was larger than I had expected. Its huge, yawning doors were menacing. I looked for Deborah and Theresa, but every face I saw was strange. I looked again at the doors of the sacred halls but I was too afraid to enter. My mother had said to go to Miss Maestas, but I did not know where to begin to find her. I had come to the town, and I had come to school, and I was very lost and afraid in the nervous, excited swarm of kids.

It was then that I felt a hand on my shoulder. I turned and looked into the eyes of a strange red-haired boy. He spoke English, a foreign tongue.

"First grade," was all I could answer. He smiled and took my hand, and with him I entered school. The building was cavernous and dark. It had strange, unfamiliar smells and sounds that seemed to gurgle from its belly. There was a big hall and many rooms, and many mothers with children passed in and out of the rooms.

I wished for my mother, but I put away the thought because I knew I was expected to become a man. A radiator snapped with steam and I jumped. The red-haired boy laughed and led me into one of the rooms. This room was brighter than the hall. So it was like this that I entered school.

Miss Maestas was a kind woman. She thanked the boy whose name was Red for bringing me in then asked my name. I told her I did not speak English.

"¡Cómo te llamas?" she asked.

"Antonio Márez," I replied. I told her my mother said I should see her, and that my mother sent her regards.

She smiled. "Anthony Márez," she wrote in a book. I drew closer to look at the letters formed by her pen. "Do you want to learn to write?" she asked.

"Yes," I answered.

"Good," she smiled.

I wanted to ask her immediately about the magic in the letters, but that would be rude and so I was quiet. I was fascinated by the black letters that formed on the paper and made my name. Miss Maestas gave me a crayon and some paper and I sat in the corner and worked at copying my name over and over. She was very busy the rest of the day with the other children that came to the room. Many cried when their mothers left, and one wet his pants. I sat in my corner alone and wrote. By noon I could write my name, and when Miss Maestas discovered that she was very pleased.

She took me to the front of the room and spoke to the other boys and girls. She pointed at me but I did not understand her. Then the other boys and girls laughed and pointed at me. I did not feel so good. Thereafter I kept away from the groups as much as I could and worked alone. I worked hard. I listened to the strange sounds. I learned new names, new words.

At noon we opened our lunches to eat. Miss Maestas left the room and a high school girl came and sat at the desk while we ate. My mother had packed a small jar of hot beans and some good, green chile wrapped in tortillas. When the other children saw my lunch they laughed and pointed again. Even the high school girl laughed. They showed me their sandwiches which were made of bread. Again I did not feel well.

I gathered my lunch and slipped out of the room. The strangeness of the school and the other children made me very sad. I did not understand them. I sneaked around the back of the school building, and standing against the wall I tried to eat. But I couldn't. A huge lump seemed to form in my throat and tears came to my eyes. I yearned for my mother, and at the same time I understood that she had sent me to this place where I was an outcast. I had tried hard to learn and they had laughed at me, I had opened my lunch to eat and again they had laughed and pointed at me.

The pain and sadness seemed to spread to my soul, and I felt for the first time what the grown-ups call *la tristesa de la vida*. I wanted to run away, to hide, to run and never come back, never see anyone again. But I knew that if I did I would shame my family name, that my mother's dream would crumble. I knew I had to grow up and be a man, but oh it was so very hard.

But no, I was not alone. Down the wall near the corner I saw two other boys who had sneaked out of the room. They were George and Willy. They were big boys, I knew they were from the farms of Delia. We banded together and in our union found strength. We found a few others who were like us, different in language and custom, and a part of our loneliness was gone. When the winter set in we moved into the auditorium and there, although many a meal was eaten in complete silence, we felt we belonged. We struggled against the feeling of loneliness that gnawed at our souls and we overcame it; that feeling I never shared again with anyone, not even with Horse and Bones, or the Kid and Samuel, or Cico or Jasón.

"Discovering Books," from *Black Boy*: A Record of Childhood and Youth

Richard Wright

*Wright, a self-educated reader with the help of his
mother, tells the story of how he managed to gain
access to books at a time when African Americans
were not allowed to check out books from libraries.
He shares how his passion for reading came to direct
his life.*

One morning I arrived early at work and went into the bank
lobby where the Negro porter was mopping. I stood at a
counter and picked up the Memphis *Commercial Appeal* and began
my free reading of the press. I came finally to the editorial page and
saw an article dealing with one H. L. Mencken. I knew by hearsay
that he was the editor of the *American Mercury*, but aside from that
I knew nothing about him. The article was a furious denunciation
of Mencken, concluding with one, hot, short sentence: Mencken is
a fool.

I wondered what on earth this Mencken had done to call down
upon him the scorn of the South. The only people I had ever heard
denounced in the South were Negroes, and this man was not a
Negro. Then what ideas did Mencken hold that made a newspaper
like the *Commercial Appeal* castigate him publicly? Undoubtedly he
must be advocating ideas that the South did not like. Were there,

then, people other than Negroes who criticized the South? I knew that during the Civil War the South had hated northern whites, but I had not encountered such hate during my life. Knowing no more of Mencken than I did at that moment, I felt a vague sympathy for him. Had not the South, which had assigned me the role of a non-man, cast at him its hardest words?

Now, how could I find out about this Mencken? There was a huge library near the riverfront, but I knew that Negroes were not allowed to patronize its shelves any more than they were the parks and playgrounds of the city. I had gone into the library several times to get books for the white men on the job. Which of them would now help me to get books? And how could I read them without causing concern to the white men with whom I worked? I had so far been successful in hiding my thoughts and feelings from them, but I knew that I would create hostility if I went about this business of reading in a clumsy way.

I weighed the personalities of the men on the job. There was Don, a Jew; but I distrusted him. His position was not much better than mine and I knew that he was uneasy and insecure; he had always treated me in an offhand, bantering way that barely concealed his contempt. I was afraid to ask him to help me to get books; his frantic desire to demonstrate a racial solidarity with the whites against Negroes might make him betray me.

Then how about the boss? No, he was a Baptist and I had the suspicion that he would not be quite able to comprehend why a black boy would want to read Mencken. There were other white men on the job whose attitudes showed clearly that they were Klux-ers or sympathizers, and they were out of the question.

There remained only one man whose attitude did not fit into an anti-Negro category, for I had heard the white men refer to him as a "Pope lover." He was an Irish Catholic and was hated by the white Southerners. I knew that he read books, because I had got him volumes from the library several times. Since he, too, was an object of hatred, I felt that he might refuse me but would hardly betray me. I hesitated, weighing and balancing the imponderable realities.

One morning I paused before the Catholic fellow's desk.

"I want to ask you a favor," I whispered to him.

"What is it?"

"I want to read. I can't get books from the library. I wonder if you'd let me use your card?"

He looked at me suspiciously.

"My card is full most of the time," he said.

"I see," I said and waited, posing my question silently.

"You're not trying to get me into trouble, are you, boy?" he asked, staring at me.

"Oh, no, sir."

"What book do you want?"

"A book by H. L. Mencken."

"Which one?"

"I don't know. Has he written more than one?"

"He has written several."

"I didn't know that."

"What makes you want to read Mencken?"

"Oh, I just saw his name in the newspaper," I said.

"It's good of you to want to read," he said. "But you ought to read the right things."

I said nothing. Would he want to supervise my reading?

"Let me think," he said. "I'll figure out something."

I turned from him and he called me back. He stared at me quizzically.

"Richard, don't mention this to the other white men," he said.

"I understand," I said. "I won't say a word."

A few days later he called me to him.

"I've got a card in my wife's name," he said. "Here's mine."

"Thank you, sir."

"Do you think you can manage it?"

"I'll manage fine," I said.

"If they suspect you, you'll get in trouble," he said.

"I'll write the same kind of notes to the library that you wrote when you sent me for books," I told him. "I'll sign your name."

He laughed.

"Go ahead. Let me see what you get," he said.

That afternoon I addressed myself to forging a note. Now, what were the names of books written by H. L. Mencken? I did not know any of them. I finally wrote what I thought would be a foolproof note: *Dear Madam: Will you please let this nigger boy*—I used the word "nigger" to make the librarian feel that I could not possibly be the author of the note—*have some books by H. L. Mencken?* I forged the white man's name.

I entered the library as I had always done when on errands for whites, but I felt that I would somehow slip up and betray myself. I doffed my hat, stood a respectful distance from the desk, looked as unbookish as possible, and waited for the white patrons to be taken care of. When the desk was clear of people, I still waited. The white librarian looked at me.

"What do you want, boy?"

As though I did not possess the power of speech, I stepped forward and simply handed her the forged note, not parting my lips.

"What books by Mencken does he want?" she asked.

"I don't know, ma'am," I said, avoiding her eyes.

"Who gave you this card?"

"Mr. Falk," I said.

"Where is he?"

"He's at work, at the M———Optical Company," I said. "I've been in here for him before."

"I remember," the woman said. "But he never wrote notes like this."

Oh, God, she's suspicious. Perhaps she would not let me have the books? If she had turned her back at that moment, I would have ducked out the door and never gone back. Then I thought of a bold idea.

"You can call him up, ma'am," I said, my heart pounding.

"You're not using these books, are you?" she asked pointedly.

"Oh, no, ma'am. I can't read."

"I don't know what he wants by Mencken," she said under her breath.

I knew now that I had won; she was thinking of other things and the race question had gone out of her mind. She went to the shelves. Once or twice she looked over her shoulder at me, as though she was still doubtful. Finally she came forward with two books in her hand.

"I'm sending him two books," she said. "But tell Mr. Falk to come in next time, or send me the names of the books he wants. I don't know what he wants to read."

I said nothing. She stamped the card and handed me the books. Not daring to glance at them, I went out of the library, fearing that the woman would call me back for further questioning. A block away from the library I opened one of the books and read a title: *A Book of Prefaces*. I was nearing my nineteenth birthday and I did not know how to pronounce the word *preface*. I thumbed the pages and saw strange words and strange names. I shook my head, disappointed. I looked at the other book; it was called *Prejudices*. I knew what that word meant; I had heard it all my life. And right off I was on guard against Mencken's books. Why would a man want to call a book *Prejudices*? The word was so stained with all my memories of racial hate that I could not conceive of anybody using it for a title. Perhaps I had made a mistake about Mencken? A man who had prejudices must be wrong.

When I showed the books to Mr. Falk, he looked at me and frowned.

"That librarian might telephone you," I warned him.

"That's all right," he said. "But when you're through reading those books, I want you to tell me what you get out of them."

That night in my rented room, while letting the hot water run over my can of pork and beans in the sink, I opened *A Book of Prefaces* and began to read. I was jarred and shocked by the style, the clear, clean, sweeping sentences. Why did he write like that? And how did one write like that? I pictured the man as a raging demon, slashing with his pen, consumed with hate, denouncing everything American, extolling everything European or German, laughing at the weaknesses of people, mocking God, authority. What was this? I stood up, trying to realize what reality lay behind the meaning of the words. . . . Yes, this man was fighting, fighting with words. He was using words as a weapon, using them as one would use a club. Could words be weapons? Well, yes, for here they were. Then, maybe, perhaps, I could use them as a weapon? No. It frightened me. I read on and what amazed me was not what he said, but how on earth anybody had the courage to say it.

Occasionally I glanced up to reassure myself that I was alone in the room. Who were these men about whom Mencken was talking so passionately? Who was Anatole France? Joseph Conrad? Sinclair Lewis, Sherwood Anderson, Dostoevski, George Moore, Gustave Flaubert, Maupassant, Tolstoy, Frank Harris, Mark Twain, Thomas Hardy, Arnold Bennett, Stephen Crane, Zola, Norris, Gorky, Bergson, Ibsen, Balzac, Bernard Shaw, Dumas, Poe, Thomas Mann, O. Henry, Dreiser, H. B. Wells, Gogol, T. S. Eliot, Gide, Baudelaire, Edgar Lee Masters, Stendhal, Turgenev, Huneker, Nietzsche, and scores of others? Were these men real? Did they exist or had they existed? And how did one pronounce their names?

I ran across many words whose meanings I did not know, and I either looked them up in a dictionary or, before I had a chance to do that, encountered the word in a context that made its meaning clear. But what strange world was this? I concluded the book with the conviction that I had somehow overlooked something terribly important in life. I had once tried to write, had once reveled in feeling, had let my crude imagination roam, but the impulse to dream had been slowly beaten out of me by experience. Now it surged up again and I hungered for books, new ways of looking and seeing. It was not a matter of believing or disbelieving what I read, but of feeling something new, of being affected by something that made the look of the world different.

As dawn broke I ate my pork and beans, feeling dopey, sleepy. I went to work, but the mood of the book would not die; it lingered, coloring everything I saw, heard, did. I now felt that I knew what the white men were feeling. Merely because I had read a book that had spoken of how they lied and thought, I identified myself with that book. I felt vaguely guilty. Would I, filled with bookish notions, act in a manner that would make the whites dislike me?

I forged more notes and my trips to the library became more frequent. Reading grew into a passion. My first serious novel was Sinclair Lewis's *Main Street*. It made me see my boss, Mr. Gerald, and identify him as an American type. I would smile when I saw him lugging his golf bags into the office. I had always felt a vast distance separating me from the boss, and now I felt closer to him, though still distant. I felt now that I knew him, that I could feel the very limits of his narrow life. And this had happened because I had read a novel about a mythical man called George F. Babbitt.

The plots and stories in the novels did not interest me so much as the point of view revealed. I gave myself over to each novel without reserve, without trying to criticize it; it was enough for me to see and feel something different. And for me, everything was something different. Reading was like a drug, a dope. The novels created moods in which I lived for days. But I could not conquer my sense of guilt, my feeling that the white men around me knew that I was changing, that I had begun to regard them differently.

Whenever I brought a book to the job, I wrapped it in newspaper—a habit that was to persist for years in other cities and under other circumstances. But some of the white men pried into my packages when I was absent and they questioned me.

"Boy, what are you reading those books for?"

"Oh, I don't know, sir."

"That's deep stuff you're reading, boy."

"I'm just killing time, sir."

"You'll addle your brains if you don't watch out."

I read Dreiser's *Jennie Gerhardt* and *Sister Carrie* and they revived in me a vivid sense of my mother's suffering; I was overwhelmed, I grew silent, wondering about the life around me. It would have been impossible for me to have told anyone what I derived from these novels, for it was nothing less than a sense of life itself. All my life had shaped me for the realism, the naturalism of the modern novel, and I could not read enough of them.

Steeped in new moods and ideas, I bought a ream of paper and tried to write; but nothing would come, or what did come was flat beyond telling. I discovered that more than desire and feeling were necessary to write and I dropped the idea. Yet I still wondered how it was possible to know people sufficiently to write about them? Could I ever learn about life and people? To me, with my vast ignorance, my Jim Crow station in life, it seemed a task impossible to achievement. I now knew what being a Negro meant. I could endure the hunger. I had learned to live with hate. But to feel that there were feelings denied me, that the very breath of life itself was beyond my reach, that more than anything else hurt, wounded me. I had a new hunger.

In buoying me up, reading also cast me down, made me see what was possible, what I had missed. My tension returned, new, terrible, bitter, surging, almost too great to be contained. I no longer *felt* that the world about me was hostile, killing; I *knew* it. A million times I asked myself what I could do to save myself, and there were no answers. I seemed forever condemned, ringed by walls.

I did not discuss my reading with Mr. Falk, who had lent me his library card; it would have meant talking about myself and that would have been too painful. I smiled each day, fighting desperately to maintain my old behavior, to keep my disposition seemingly sunny. But some of the white men discerned that I had begun to brood.

"Wake up there, boy!" Mr. Olin said one day.

"Sir!" I answered for the lack of a better word.

"You act like you've stolen something," he said.

I laughed in the way I knew he expected me to laugh, but I resolved to be more conscious of myself, to watch my every act, to guard and hide the new knowledge that was dawning within me.

If I went north, would it be possible for me to build a new life then? But how could a man build a life upon vague, unformed yearnings? I wanted to write and I did not even know the English language. I bought English grammars and found them dull. I felt that I was getting a better sense of the language from novels than grammars. I read hard, discarding a writer as soon as I felt that I had grasped his point of view. At night the printed page stood before my eyes in sleep.

Mrs. Moss, my landlady, asked me one Sunday morning:

"Son, what is this you keep on reading?"

"Oh, nothing. Just novels."

"What you get out of 'em?"

"I'm just killing time," I said.

"I hope you know your own mind," she said in a tone which implied that she doubted if I had a mind.

I knew of no Negroes who read the books I liked and I wondered if any Negroes ever thought of them. I knew that there were Negro doctors, lawyers, newspapermen, but I never saw any of them. When I read a Negro newspaper I never caught the faintest echo of my preoccupation in its pages. I felt trapped and occasionally, for a few days, I would stop reading. But a vague hunger would come over me for books, books that opened up new avenues of feeling and seeing, and again I would forge another note to the white librarian. Again I would read and wonder as only the naïve and unlettered can read and wonder, feeling that I carried a secret, criminal burden about with me each day.

That winter my mother and brother came and we set up housekeeping, buying furniture on the installment plan, being cheated and yet knowing no way to avoid it. I began to eat warm food and to my surprise found the regular meals enabled me to read faster. I may have lived through many illnesses and survived them, never suspecting that I was ill. My brother obtained a job and we began to save toward the trip north, plotting our time, setting tentative dates for departure. I told none of the white men on the job that I was planning to go north; I knew that the moment they felt I was thinking of the North they would change toward me. It would have made them feel that I did not like the life I was living, and because my life was completely conditioned by what they said or did, it would have been tantamount to challenging them.

I could calculate my chances for life in the South as a Negro fairly clearly now.

I could fight the southern whites by organizing with other Negroes, as my grandfather had done. But I knew that I could never win that way; there are many whites and there were but few blacks. They were strong and we were weak. Outright black rebellion could never win. If I fought openly I would die and I did not want to die. News of lynchings were frequent.

I could submit and live the life of a genial slave, but that was impossible. All of my life had shaped me to live by my own feelings and thoughts. I could make up to Bess and marry her and inherit the house. But that, too, would be the life of a slave; if I did that, I would crush to death something within me, and I would hate myself as much as I knew the whites already hated those who had submitted. Neither could I ever willingly present myself to be kicked, as Shorty had done. I would rather have died than do that.

I could drain off my restlessness by fighting with Shorty and Harrison. I had seen many Negroes solve the problem of being black by transferring their hatred of themselves to others with a black skin and fighting them. I would have to be cold to do that, and I was not cold and I could never be.

I could, of course, forget what I had read, thrust the whites out of my mind, forget them; and find release from anxiety and longing in sex and alcohol. But the memory of how my father had conducted himself made that course repugnant. If I did not want others to violate my life, how could I voluntarily violate it myself?

I had no hope whatever of being a professional man. Not only had I been so conditioned that I did not desire it, but the fulfillment of such an ambition was beyond my capabilities. Well-to-do Negroes lived in a world that was almost as alien to me as the world inhabited by whites.

What, then, was there? I held my life in my mind, in my consciousness each day, feeling at times that I would stumble and drop it, spill it forever. My reading had created a vast sense of distance between me and the world in which I lived and tried to make a living, and that sense of distance was increasing each day. My days and nights were one long, quiet, continuously contained dream of terror, tension, and anxiety. I wondered how long I could bear it.

8

"The Gift of Reading," from *Better Than Life*

Daniel Pennac

*A high school teacher defies and surprises his stu-
dents, especially those who say they don't like to read.
He tells his students to relax, and put away the pens
and paper; there will be no comprehension test. And
then, in the face of their surprise and negativity, he
begins to read out loud.*

Of course, they don't like to read. Too much vocabulary in
books. Too many pages, too. Too many books, when it comes
down to it.

No, definitely, they don't like to read.

That's what the raised hands suggest when the teacher asks,
"Who here doesn't like to read?"

Nearly all the hands go up. That's a challenge in itself. A few
aren't raised (the Anorexic's, among others), but that's out of sheer
indifference to the question.

"In that case," says the teacher, "since you don't like to read, I'll
read you the books myself."

With no further ado, he opens his bag and takes out an enormous book, a regular doorstop, a brick with a glossy cover. The most
bookish-looking book you could imagine.

"Are you ready?"

They don't believe their eyes or their ears. Is he going to read them *all* that? It'll take him all year! They're confused. The atmosphere is tense. There's no such thing as a teacher who spends the whole year reading. Either he's lazier than they are, or he's got something up his sleeve. This is some kind of trap. There's got to be a daily vocabulary list and a comprehension test at the end.

The students glance at each other. A few of them just in case, take out a sheet of paper and prepare their ballpoints.

"Don't bother taking notes. Just try to listen, that's all."

Now comes the problem of *attitude*. What do you do with your body in a classroom without the props of a ballpoint pen and a sheet of lined paper? What do you do with yourself under such circumstances?

"Sit back, make yourself comfortable, relax."

Relax? That's a good one!

Curiosity gains the upper hand. The Punks ask, "You're going to read us that whole book . . . *out loud?*"

"I don't see how you could hear me if I read it to myself."

Discreet laughter. The Anorexic doesn't go for that bait. In a stage whisper heard by everyone, she declares, "We're too old for that kind of stuff."

That's the usual prejudice among those who have never been given the gift of reading. The rest of us know you're never too old for that pleasure.

"If, in ten minutes, you still think you're too old, raise your hand and we'll go on to something else, okay?"

"What kind of book is it?" Reebok asks, as if he'd read them all.

"A novel."

"What's it about?"

"It's hard to say if you haven't read it. All right, are you ready? That's enough talk. Let's hit it."

They're skeptical, but willing to try.

"*In eighteenth-century France there lived a man who was one of the most gifted and abominable personalities in an era that knew no lack of gifted and abominable personages . . .*"

"Coming into Language," from *Doing Time: Twenty-Five Years of Prison Writing*

Jimmy Santiago Baca

Baca, unable to read at age seventeen and a high school dropout, remembers a picture book about his Latino culture that once captured his attention. Two years later, in jail, he steals a book from an unattentive warden—a book that becomes, to his surprise, the catalyst for his journey toward reading and writing.

On weekend graveyard shifts at St. Joseph's Hospital I worked the emergency room, mopping up pools of blood and carting plastic bags stuffed with arms, legs, and hands to the outdoor incinerator. I enjoyed the quiet, away from the screams of shotgunned, knifed, and mangled kids writhing on gurneys outside the operating rooms. Ambulance sirens shrieked and squad car lights reddened the cool nights, flashing against the hospital walls: gray—red, gray—red. On slow nights I would lock the door of the administration office, search the reference library for a book on female anatomy and, with my feet propped on the desk, leaf through the illustrations, smoking my cigarette. I was seventeen.

One night my eye was caught by a familiar-looking word on the spine of a book. The title was *450 Years of Chicano History in Pictures*. On the cover were black-and-white photos: Padre Hidalgo exhorting Mexican peasants to revolt against the Spanish dictators;

Anglo vigilantes hanging two Mexicans from a tree; a young Mexican woman with rifle and ammunition belts crisscrossing her breast; César Chávez and field workers marching for fair wages; Chicano railroad workers laying creosote ties; Chicanas laboring at machines in textile factories; Chicanas picketing and hoisting boycott signs.

From the time I was seven, teachers had been punishing me for not knowing my lessons by making me stick my nose in a circle chalked on the blackboard. Ashamed of not understanding and fearful of asking questions, I dropped out of school in the ninth grade. At seventeen I still didn't know how to read, but those pictures confirmed my identity. I stole the book that night, stashing it for safety under the slop sink until I got off work. Back at my boardinghouse, I showed the book to friends. All of us were amazed; this book told us we were alive. We, too, had defended ourselves with our fists against hostile Anglos, gasping for breath in fights with the policemen who outnumbered us. The book reflected back to us our struggle in a way that made us proud.

Most of my life I felt like a target in the crosshairs of a hunter's rifle. When strangers and outsiders questioned me I felt the hangrope tighten around my neck and the trapdoor creak beneath my feet. There was nothing so humiliating as being unable to express myself, and my inarticulateness increased my sense of jeopardy. Behind a mask of humility, I seethed with mute rebellion.

Before I was eighteen, I was arrested on suspicion of murder after refusing to explain a deep cut on my forearm. With shocking speed I found myself handcuffed to a chain gang of inmates and bused to a holding facility to await trial. There I met men, prisoners, who read aloud to each other the works of Neruda, Paz, Sabines, Nemerov, and Hemingway. Never had I felt such freedom as in that dormitory. Listening to the words of these writers, I felt that invisible threat from without lessen—my sense of teetering on a rotting plank over swamp water where famished alligators clapped their horny snouts for my blood. While I listened to the words of the poets, the alligators slumbered powerless in their lairs. The language of poetry was the magic that could liberate me from myself, transform me into another person, transport me to places far away.

And when they closed the books, these Chicanos, and went into their own Chicano language, they made barrio life come alive for me in the fullness of its vitality. I began to learn my own language, the bilingual words and phrases explaining to me my place in the universe.

Months later I was released, as I had suspected I would be. I had been guilty of nothing but shattering the windshield of my girlfriend's car in a fit of rage.

Two years passed. I was twenty now, and behind bars again. The federal marshals had failed to provide convincing evidence to extradite me to Arizona on a drug charge, but still I was being held. They had ninety days to prove I was guilty. The only evidence against me was that my girlfriend had been at the scene of the crime with my driver's license in her purse. They had to come up with something else. But there was nothing else. Eventually they negotiated a deal with the actual drug dealer, who took the stand against me. When the judge hit me with a million-dollar bail, I emptied my pockets on his booking desk: twenty-six cents.

One night in my third month in the county jail, I was mopping the floor in front of the booking desk. Some detectives had kneed an old drunk and handcuffed him to the booking bars. His shrill screams raked my nerves like a hacksaw on bone, the desperate protest of his dignity against their inhumanity. But the detectives just laughed as he tried to rise and kicked him to his knees. When they went to the bathroom to pee and the desk attendant walked to the file cabinet to pull the arrest record, I shot my arm through the bars, grabbed one of the attendant's university textbooks, and tucked it in my overalls. It was the only way I had of protesting.

It was late when I returned to my cell. Under my blanket I switched on a pen flashlight and opened the thick book at random, scanning the pages. I could hear the jailer making his rounds on the other tiers. The jangle of his keys and the sharp click of his boot

heels intensified my solitude. Slowly I enunciated the words . . .
p-o-n-d, ri-pple. It scared me that I had been reduced to this to find
comfort. I always had thought reading a waste of time, that nothing could be gained by it. Only by action, by moving out into the
world and confronting and challenging the obstacles, could one
learn anything worth knowing.

Even as I tried to convince myself that I was merely curious, I
became so absorbed in how the sounds created music in me and
happiness, I forgot where I was. Memories began to quiver in me,
glowing with a strange but familiar intimacy in which I found ref-
uge. For a while, a deep sadness overcame me, as if I had chanced
on a long-lost friend and mourned the years of separation. But soon
the heartache of having missed so much of life, that had numbed
me since I was a child, gave way, as if a grave illness lifted itself from
me and I was cured, innocently believing in the beauty of life again.
I stumblingly repeated the author's name as I fell asleep, saying it
over and over in the dark: Words-worth, Words-worth.

Before long my sister came to visit me, and I joked about taking
her to a place called Xanadu and getting her a blind date with this
vato ["dude," in Chicano dialect] named Coleridge who lived on the
seacoast and was *malias* ["strung out," in Chicano dialect] on mor-
phine. When I asked her to make a trip into enemy territory to buy
me a grammar book, she said she couldn't. Bookstores intimidated
her, because she, too, could neither read nor write.

Days later, with a stub pencil I whittled sharp with my teeth, I
propped a Red Chief notebook on my knees and wrote my first
words. From that moment, a hunger for poetry possessed me.

Until then, I had felt as if I had been born into a raging ocean
where I swam relentlessly, flailing my arms in hope of rescue, of
reaching a shoreline I never sighted. Never solid ground beneath
me, never a resting place. I had lied with only the desperate hope
to stay afloat; that and nothing more.

But when at last I wrote my first words on the page, I felt an
island rising beneath my feet like the back of a whale. As more and

more words emerged, I could finally rest: I had a place to stand for the first time in my life. The island grew, with each page, into a continent inhabited by people I knew and mapped with the life I lived.

I wrote about it all—about people I had loved or hated, about the brutalities and ecstasies of my life. And, for the first time, the child in me who had witnessed and endured unspeakable terrors cried out not just in impotent despair, but with the power of language. Suddenly, through language, through writing, my grief and my joy could be shared with anyone who would listen. And I could do this all alone; I could do it anywhere. I was no longer a captive of demons eating away at me, no longer a victim of other people's mockery and loathing, that had made me clench my fist white with rage and grit my teeth to silence. Words now pleaded back with the bleak lucidity of hurt. They were wrong, those others, and now I could say it.

Through language I was free. I could respond, escape, indulge; embrace or reject earth or the cosmos. I was launched on an endless journey without boundaries or rules, in which I could salvage the floating fragments of my past, or be born anew in the spontaneous ignition of understanding some heretofore concealed aspect of myself. Each word steamed with the hot lava juices of my primordial making, and I crawled out of stanzas dripping with birthblood, reborn and freed from the chaos of my life. The child in the dark room of my heart, who had never been able to find or reach the light switch, flicked it on now; and I found in the room a stranger, myself, who had waited so many years to speak again. My words struck in me lightning crackles of elation and thunderhead storms of grief.

When I had been in the county jail longer than anyone else, I was made a trustee. One morning, after a fistfight, I went to the unlocked and unoccupied office used for lawyer-client meetings, to think. The bare white room with its fluorescent tube lighting seemed to expose and illuminate my dark and worthless life. When I had fought before,

I never gave it a thought. Now, for the first time, I had something to lose—my chance to read, to write; a way to live with dignity and meaning, that had opened for me when I stole that scuffed, second-hand book about the Romantic poets.

"I will never do any work in this prison system as long as I am not allowed to get my G.E.D." That's what I told the reclassification panel. The captain flicked off the tape recorder. He looked at me hard and said, "You'll never walk outta here alive. Oh, you'll work, put a copper penny on that, you'll work."

After that interview I was confined to deadlock maximum security in a subterranean dungeon, with ground-level chicken-wired windows painted gray. Twenty-three hours a day I was in that cell. I kept sane by borrowing books from the other cons on the tier. Then, just before Christmas, I received a letter from Harry, a charity house Samaritan who doled out hot soup to the homeless in Phoenix. He had picked my name from a list of cons who had no one to write to them. I wrote back asking for a grammar book, and a week later received one of Mary Baker Eddy's treatises on salvation and redemption, with Spanish and English on opposing pages. Pacing my cell all day and most of each night, I grappled with grammar until I was able to write a long true-romance confession for a con to send to his pen pal. He paid me with a pack of smokes. Soon I had a thriving barter business, exchanging my poems and letters for novels, commissary pencils, and writing tablets.

One day I tore two flaps from the cardboard box that held all my belongings and punctured holes along the edge of each flap and along the border of a ream of state-issue paper. After I had aligned them to form a spine, I threaded the holes with a shoestring, and sketched on the cover a hummingbird fluttering above a rose. This was my first journal.

Whole afternoons I wrote, unconscious of passing time or whether it was day or night. Sunbursts exploded from the lead tip of my pencil, words that grafted me into awareness of who I was; peeled back to a burning core of bleak terror, an embryo floating in the image of water, I cracked out of the shell wide-eyed and insane. Trees grew out of the palms of my hands, the threatening otherness of life dissolved, and I became one with the air and sky, the dirt and the iron and concrete. There was no longer any distinction between the other and I. Language made bridges of fire between me and everything I saw. I entered into the blade of grass, the basketball, and con's eye and child's soul.

At night I flew. I conversed with floating heads in my cell, and visited strange houses where lonely women brewed tea and rocked in wicker rocking chairs listening to sad Joni Mitchell songs.

Before long I was frayed like rope carrying too much weight, that suddenly snaps. I quit talking. Bars, walls, steel bunk and floor bristled with millions of poem-making sparks. My face was no longer familiar to me. The only reality was the swirling cornucopia of images in my mind, the voices in the air. Midair a cactus blossom would appear, a snake-flame in blinding dance around it, stunning me like a guard's fist striking my neck from behind.

The prison administrators tried several tactics to get me to work. For six months, after the next monthly prison board review, they sent cons to my cell to hassle me. When the guard would open my cell door to let one of them in, I'd leap out and fight him—and get sent to thirty-day isolation. I did a lot of isolation time. But I honed my image-making talents in that sensory-deprived solitude. Finally they moved me to death row, and after that to "nut-run," the tier that housed the mentally disturbed.

As the months passed, I became more and more sluggish. My eyelids were heavy, I could no longer write or read. I slept all the time.

One day a guard took me out to the exercise field. For the first time in years I felt grass and earth under my feet. It was spring. The sun warmed my face as I sat on the bleachers watching the cons box and run, hit the handball, lift weights. Some of them stopped to ask how I was, but I found it impossible to utter a syllable. My tongue would not move, saliva drooled from the corners of my mouth. I had been so heavily medicated I could not summon the slightest gestures.

Yet inside me a small voice cried out, I am fine! I am hurt now but I will come back! I'm fine!

Back in my cell, for weeks I refused to eat. Styrofoam cups of urine and hot water were hurled at me. Other things happened. There were beatings, shock therapy, intimidation.

Later, I regained some clarity of mind. But there was a place in my heart where I had died. My life had compressed itself into an unbearable dread of being. The strain had been too much. I had stepped over that line where a human being has lost more than he can bear, where the pain is too intense, and he knows he is changed forever. I was now capable of killing, coldly and without feeling. I was empty, as I have never, before or since, known emptiness. I had no connection to this life.

But then, the encroaching darkness that began to envelop me forced me to re-form and give birth to myself again in the chaos. I withdrew even deeper into the world of language, cleaving the dia-monds of verbs and nouns, plunging into the brilliant light of poetry's regenerative mystery. Words gave off rings of white energy, radar signals from powers beyond me that infused me with truth. I believed what I wrote, because I wrote what was true. My words did not come from books or textual formulas, but from a deep faith in the voice of my heart.

I had been steeped in self-loathing and rejected by everyone and everything—society, family, cons, God and demons. But now I had become as the burning ember floating in darkness that descends on a dry leaf and sets flame to forests. The word was the ember and the forest was my life. . . .

Writing bridged my divided life of prisoner and free man. I wrote of the emotional butchery of prisons, and my acute gratitude for poetry. Where my blind doubt and spontaneous trust in life met, I discovered empathy and compassion. The power to express myself was a welcome storm rasping at tendril roots, flooding my soul's cracked dirt. Writing was water that cleansed the wound and fed the parched root of my heart.

I wrote to sublimate my rage, from a place where all hope is gone, from a madness of having been damaged too much, from a silence of killing rage. I wrote to avenge the betrayals of a lifetime, to purge the bitterness of injustice. I wrote with a deep groan of doom in my blood, bewildered and dumbstruck; from an indestructible love of life, to affirm breath and laughter and the abiding innocence of things. I wrote the way I wept, and danced, and made love.

10

"Silence," from *Woman Warrior*

Maxine Hong Kingston

*"Silence" describes a young girl's reaction to her
American schooling. The girl's mother has cut her
daughter's tongue shortly after she is born, driven by
her desire for her daughter to be able to speak many
languages in her new land. The young girl, however,
breaks the silence in only one language.*

Long ago in China, knot-makers tied string into buttons and
frogs, and rope into bell pulls. There was one knot so complicated that it blinded the knot-maker. Finally an emperor outlawed
this cruel knot, and the nobles could not order it anymore. If I had
lived in China, I would have been an outlaw knot-maker.

Maybe that's why my mother cut my tongue. She pushed my
tongue up and sliced the frenum. Or maybe she snipped it with a
pair of nail scissors. I don't remember her doing it, only her telling
me about it, but all during childhood I felt sorry for the baby whose
mother waited with scissors or knife in hand for it to cry—and then,
when its mouth was wide open like a baby bird's, cut. The Chinese
say "a ready tongue is an evil."

I used to curl up my tongue in front of the mirror and tauten my
frenum into a white line, itself as thin as a razor blade. I saw no scars
in my mouth. I thought perhaps I had had two frena, and she had cut
one. I made other children open their mouths so I could compare

theirs to mine. I saw perfect pink membranes stretching into precise edges that looked easy enough to cut. Sometimes I felt very proud that my mother committed such a powerful act upon me. At other times I was terrified—the first thing my mother did when she saw me was to cut my tongue.

"Why did you do that to me, Mother?"

"I told you."

"Tell me again."

"I cut it so that you would not be tongue-tied. Your tongue would be able to move in any language. You'll be able to speak languages that are completely different from one another. You'll be able to pronounce anything. Your frenum looked too tight to do those things, so I cut it."

"But isn't 'a ready tongue an evil'?"

"Things are different in this ghost country."

"Did it hurt me? Did I cry and bleed?"

"I don't remember. Probably."

She didn't cut the other children's. When I asked cousins and other Chinese children whether their mothers had cut their tongues loose, they said, "What?"

"Why didn't you cut my brothers' and sisters' tongues?"

"They didn't need it."

"Why not? Were theirs longer than mine?"

"Why don't you quit blabbering and get to work?"

If my mother was not lying she should have cut more, scraped away the rest of the frenum skin, because I have a terrible time talking. Or she should not have cut at all, tampering with my speech. When I went to kindergarten and had to speak English for the first time, I became silent. A dumbness—a shame—still cracks my voice in two, even when I want to say "hello" casually, or ask an easy question in front of the check-out counter, or ask directions of a bus driver. I stand frozen, or I hold up the line with the complete, grammatical sentence that comes squeaking out at impossible length. "What did you say?" says the cab driver, or "Speak up," so I have to perform again, only weaker the second time. A telephone call makes my throat bleed and takes up that day's courage. It spoils my day with self-disgust when I hear my broken voice come skittering out into the open. It makes people wince to hear it. I'm getting better, though. Recently I asked the postman for special-issue stamps; I've waited since childhood for postmen to give me some of their own accord. I am making progress, a little every day.

My silence was thickest—total—during the three years that I covered my school paintings with black paint. I painted layers of black over houses and flowers and suns, and when I drew on the blackboard, I put a layer of chalk on top. I was making a stage curtain, and it was the moment before the curtain parted or rose. The teachers called my parents to school, and I saw they had been saving my pictures, curling and cracking, all alike and black. The teachers pointed to the pictures and looked serious, talked seriously too, but my parents did not understand English. ("The parents and teachers of criminals were executed," said my father.) My parents took the pictures home. I spread them out (so black and full of possibilities) and pretended the curtains were swinging open, flying up, one after another, sunlight underneath, mighty operas.

During the first silent year I spoke to no one at school, did not ask before going to the lavatory, and flunked kindergarten. My sister also said nothing for three years, silent in the playground and silent at lunch. There were other quiet Chinese girls not of our family, but most of them got over it sooner than we did. I enjoyed the silence. At first it did not occur to me I was supposed to talk or to pass kindergarten. I talked at home and to one or two of the Chinese kids in the class. I made motions and even made some jokes. I drank out of a toy saucer when the water spilled out of the cup, and everybody laughed, pointing at me, so I did it some more. I didn't know that Americans don't drink out of saucers.

I liked the Negro students (Black Ghosts) best because they laughed the loudest and talked to me as if I were a daring talker too. One of the Negro girls had her mother coil braids over her ears

Shanghai-style like mine; we were Shanghai twins except that she was covered with black like my paintings. Two Negro kids enrolled in Chinese school, and the teachers gave them Chinese names. Some Negro kids walked me to school and home, protecting me from the Japanese kids, who hit me and chased me and stuck gum in my ears. The Japanese kids were noisy and tough. They appeared one day in kindergarten, released from concentration camp, which was a tic-tac-toe mark, like barbed wire, on the map.

It was when I found out I had to talk that school became a misery, that the silence became a misery. I did not speak and felt bad each time that I did not speak. I read aloud in first grade, though, and heard the barest whisper with little squeaks come out of my throat. "Louder," said the teacher, who scared the voice away again. The other Chinese girls did not talk either, so I knew the silence had to do with being a Chinese girl.

Reading out loud was easier than speaking because we did not have to make up what to say, but I stopped often, and the teacher would think I'd gone quiet again. I could not understand "I." The Chinese "I" has seven strokes, intricacies. How could the American "I," assuredly wearing a hat like the Chinese, have only three strokes, the middle so straight? Was it out of politeness that this writer left off strokes the way a Chinese has to write her own name small and crooked? No, it was not politeness; "I" is a capital and "you" is a lower-case. I stared at that middle line and waited so long for its black center to resolve into tight strokes and dots that I forgot to pronounce it. The other troublesome word was "here," no strong consonant to hang on to, and so flat, when "here" is two mountainous ideographs. The teacher, who had told me every day how to read "I" and "here," put me in the low corner under the stairs again, where the noisy boys usually sat.

When my second grade class did a play, the whole class went to the auditorium except the Chinese girls. The teacher, lovely and Hawaiian, should have understood about us, but instead left us behind in the classroom. Our voices were too soft or nonexistent, and our parents never signed the permission slips anyway. They never signed anything unnecessary. We opened the door a crack and peeked out, but closed it again quickly. One of us (not me) won every spelling bee, though.

I remember telling the Hawaiian teacher, "We Chinese can't sing 'land where our fathers died.'" She argued with me about politics, while I meant because of curses. But how can I have that memory when I couldn't talk? My mother says that we, like the ghosts, have no memories.

After American school, we picked up our cigar boxes, in which we had arranged books, brushes, and an inkbox neatly, and went to Chinese school, from 5:00 to 7:30 P.M. There we chanted together, voices rising and falling, loud and soft, some boys shouting, everybody reading together, reciting together and not alone with one voice. When we had a memorization test, the teacher let each of us come to his desk and say the lesson to him privately, while the rest of the class practiced copying or tracing. Most of the teachers were men. The boys who were so well behaved in the American school played tricks on them and talked back to them. The girls were not mute. They screamed and yelled during recess, when there were no rules; they had fistfights. Nobody was afraid of children hurting themselves or of children hurting school property. The glass doors to the red and green balconies with the gold joy symbols were left wide open so that we could run out and climb the fire escapes. We played capture-the-flag in the auditorium, where Sun Yat-sen and Chiang Kai-shek's pictures hung at the back of the stage, the Chinese flag on their left and the American flag on their right. We climbed the teak ceremonial chairs and made flying leaps off the stage. One flag headquarters was behind the glass door and the other on stage right. Our feet drummed on the hollow stage. During recess the teachers locked themselves up in their office with the shelves of books, copybooks, inks from China. They drank tea and warmed their hands at a stove. There was no play supervision. At recess we had the school to ourselves, and also we could roam as far as we could go—downtown, Chinatown stores, home—as long as we returned before the bell rang.

At exactly 7:30 the teacher again picked up the brass bell that sat on his desk and swung it over our heads, while we charged down the stairs, our cheering magnified in the stairwell. Nobody had to line up.

Not all of the children who were silent at American school found voice at Chinese school. One new teacher said each of us had to get up and recite in front of the class, who was to listen. My sister and I had memorized the lesson perfectly. We said it to each other at home, one chanting, one listening. The teacher called on my sister to recite first. It was the first time a teacher had called on the second-born to go first. My sister was scared. She glanced at me and looked away; I looked down at my desk. I hoped that she could do it because if she could, then I would have to. She opened her mouth and a voice came out that wasn't a whisper, but it wasn't a proper voice either. I hoped that she would not cry, fear breaking up her voice like twigs underfoot. She sounded as if she were trying to sing through weeping and strangling. She did not pause or stop to end the embarrassment. She kept going until she said the last word, and then she sat down. When it was my turn, the same voice came out, a crippled animal running on broken legs. You could hear splinters in my voice, bones rubbing jagged against one another. I was loud, though. I was glad I didn't whisper. There was one little girl who whispered.

11

"Aria: A Memoir of a Bilingual Childhood," from *Hunger of Memory: The Education of Richard Rodriguez*

Richard Rodriguez

Rodriguez describes the two language and cultural worlds of Spanish and English that he experienced as a young child. Spanish provided him with the safety and security of home; English was the language of school and social status. As he strives to learn English, he realizes that he has sacrificed his native language and culture in the process.

I remember, to start with, that day in Sacramento, in a California now nearly thirty years past, when I first entered a classroom—able to understand about fifty stray English words. The third of four children, I had been preceded by my older brother and sister to a neighborhood Roman Catholic school. But neither of them had revealed very much about their classroom experiences. They left each morning and returned each afternoon, always together, speaking Spanish as they climbed the five steps to the porch. And their mysterious books, wrapped in brown shopping-bag paper, remained on the table next to the door, closed firmly behind them.

An accident of geography sent me to a school where all my classmates were white and many were the children of doctors and lawyers and business executives. On that first day of school, my classmates must certainly have been uneasy to find themselves apart from their families, in the first institution of their lives. But I was astonished. I was fated to be the "problem student" in class.

The nun said, in a friendly but oddly impersonal voice: "Boys and girls, this is Richard Rodriguez." (I heard her sound it out: *Rich-heard Road-ree-guess.*) It was the first time I had heard anyone say my name in English. "Richard," the nun repeated more slowly, writing my name down in her book. Quickly I turned to see my mother's face dissolve in a watery blur behind the pebbled-glass door.

Now, many years later, I hear of something called "bilingual education"—a scheme proposed in the late 1960s by Hispanic-American social activists, later endorsed by a congressional vote. It is a program that seeks to permit non-English-speaking children (many from lower class homes) to use their "family language" as the language of school. Such, at least, is the aim its supporters announce. I hear them, and am forced to say no: It is not possible for a child, any child, ever to use his family's language in school. Not to understand this is to misunderstand the public uses of schooling and to trivialize the nature of intimate life.

Memory teaches me what I know of these matters. The boy reminds the adult. I was a bilingual child, but of a certain kind: "socially disadvantaged," the son of working-class parents, both Mexican immigrants.

In the early years of my boyhood, my parents coped very well in America. My father had steady work. My mother managed at home. They were nobody's victims. When we moved to a house many blocks from the Mexican-American section of town, they were not intimidated by those two or three neighbors who initially tried to make us unwelcome. ("Keep your brats away from my sidewalk!") But despite all they achieved, or perhaps because they had so much to achieve, they lacked any deep feeling of ease, of belonging in public. They regarded the people at work or in crowds as being very distant from us. Those were the others, *los gringos*. That term was interchangeable in their speech with another, even more telling: *los americanos*.

I grew up in a house where the only regular guests were my relations. On a certain day, enormous families of relatives would visit
us, and there would be so many people that the noise and the bodies would spill out to the backyard and onto the front porch. Then
for weeks no one would come. (If the doorbell rang, it was usually
a salesman.) Our house stood apart—gaudy yellow in a row of white
bungalows. We were the people with the noisy dog, the people who
raised chickens. We were the foreigners on the block. A few neighbors would smile and wave at us. We waved back. But until I was
seven years old, I did not know the name of the old couple living
next door or the names of the kids living across the street.

In public, my father and mother spoke a hesitant, accented, and
not always grammatical English. And then they would have to
strain, their bodies tense, to catch the sense of what was rapidly said
by *los gringos*. At home, they returned to Spanish. The language of
their Mexican past sounded in counterpoint to the English spoken
in public. The words would come quickly, with ease. Conveyed
through those sounds was the pleasing, soothing, consoling
reminder that one was at home.

During those years when I was first learning to speak, my mother
and father addressed me only in Spanish; in Spanish I learned to
reply. By contrast, English (*inglés*) was the language I came to asso-
ciate with gringos, rarely heard in the house. I learned my first words
of English overhearing my parents speaking to strangers. At six years
of age, I knew just enough words for my mother to trust me on
errands to stores one block away—but no more.

I was then a listening child, careful to hear the very different
sounds of Spanish and English. Wide-eyed with hearing, I'd listen
to sounds more than to words. First, there were English (gringo)
sounds. So many words still were unknown to me that when the
butcher or the lady at the drugstore said something, exotic polysyl-
labic sounds would bloom in the midst of their sentences. Often the
speech of people in public seemed to me very loud, booming with
confidence. The man behind the counter would literally ask, "What

can I do for you?" But by being so firm and clear, the sound of his voice said that he was a gringo; he belonged in public society. There were also the high, nasal notes of middle-class American speech—which I rarely am conscious of hearing today because I hear them so often, but could not stop hearing when I was a boy. Crowds at Safeway or at bus stops were noisy with the birdlike sounds of *los gringos*. I'd move away from them all—all the chirping chatter above me.

My own sounds I was unable to hear, but I knew that I spoke English poorly. My words could not extend to form complete thoughts. And the words I did speak I didn't know well enough to make distinct sounds. (Listeners would usually lower their heads to hear better what I was trying to say.) But it was one thing for *me* to speak English with difficulty; it was more troubling to hear my parents speaking in public: their high-whining vowels and guttural consonants; their sentences that got stuck with "eh" and "ah" sounds; the confused syntax; the hesitant rhythm of sounds so different from the way gringos spoke. I'd notice, moreover, that my parents' voices were softer than those of gringos we would meet.

I am tempted to say now that none of this mattered. (In adulthood I am embarrassed by childhood fears.) And, in a way, it didn't matter very much that my parents could not speak English with ease. Their linguistic difficulties had no serious consequences. My mother and father made themselves understood at the county hospital clinic and at government offices. And yet, in another way, it mattered very much. It was unsettling to hear my parents struggle with English. Hearing them, I'd grow nervous, and my clutching trust in their protection and power would be weakened.

There were many times like the night at a brightly lit gasoline station (a blaring white memory) when I stood uneasily hearing my father talk to a teenage attendant. I do not recall what they were saying, but I cannot forget the sounds my father made as he spoke. At one point his words slid together to form one long word—sounds as confused as the threads of blue and green oil in the puddle next to my shoes. His voice rushed through what he had left to say. Toward the end, he reached falsetto notes, appealing to his listener's understanding. I looked away at the lights of passing automobiles. I tried not to hear any more. But I heard only too well the attendant's reply, his calm, easy tones. Shortly afterward, headed for home, I shivered when my father put his hand on my shoulder. The very first chance that I got, I evaded his grasp and ran on ahead into the dark, skipping with feigned boyish exuberance.

But then there was Spanish: *español*, the language rarely heard away from the house; *español*, the language which seemed to me therefore a private language, my family's language. To hear its sounds was to feel myself specially recognized as one of the family, apart from *los otros*. A simple remark, an inconsequential comment could convey that assurance. My parents would say something to me and I would feel embraced by the sounds of their words. Those sounds said: *I am speaking with ease in Spanish. I am addressing you in words I never use with los gringos. I recognize you as someone special, close, like no one outside. You belong with us. In the family. Ricardo.*

At the age of six, well past the time when most middle-class children no longer notice the difference between sounds uttered at home and words spoken in public, I had a different experience. I lived in a world compounded of sounds. I was a child longer than most. I lived in a magical world, surrounded by sounds both pleasing and fearful. I shared with my family a language enchantingly private—different from that used in the city around us.

Just opening or closing the screen door behind me was an important experience. I'd rarely leave home all alone or without feeling reluctance. Walking down the sidewalk, under the canopy of tall trees, I'd warily notice the (suddenly) silent neighborhood kids who stood warily watching me. Nervously, I'd arrive at the grocery store to hear there the sounds of the gringo, reminding me that in this so-big world I was a foreigner. But if leaving home was never routine, neither was coming back. Walking toward our house, climbing the steps from the sidewalk, in summer when the front door was open, I'd hear voices beyond the screen door talking in Spanish. For a second or two I'd stay, linger there listening. Smiling, I'd hear my mother call out, saying in Spanish, "Is that you, Richard?" Those were her words, but all the while her sounds would assure me: *You are home now. Come closer inside. With us.* "*Sí,*" I'd reply.

Once more inside the house, I would resume my place in the family. The sounds would grow harder to hear. Once more at home, I would grow less conscious of them. It required, however, no more than the blurt of the doorbell to alert me all over again to listen to sounds. The house would turn instantly quiet while my mother went to the door. I'd hear her hard English sounds. I'd wait to hear her voice turn to soft-sounding Spanish, which assured me, as surely as did the clicking tongue of the lock on the door, that the stranger was gone.

Plainly it is not healthy to hear such sounds so often. It is not healthy to distinguish public from private sounds so easily. I remained cloistered by sounds, timid and shy in public, too dependent on the voices at home. And yet I was a very happy child when I was at home. I remember many nights when my father would come back from work, and I'd hear him call out to my mother in Spanish, sounding relieved. In Spanish, his voice would sound the light and free notes that he never could manage in English. Some nights I'd jump up just hearing his voice. My brother and I would come running into the room where he was with our mother. Our laughing (so deep was the pleasure!) became screaming. Like others who feel the pain of public alienation, we transformed the knowledge of our public separateness into a consoling reminder of our intimacy. Excited, our voices joined in a celebration of sounds. *We are speaking now the way we never speak out in public—we are together,* the sounds told me. Some nights no one seemed willing to loosen the hold that sounds had on us. At dinner we invented new words that sounded Spanish, but made sense only to us. We pieced together new words by taking, say, an English verb and giving it Spanish endings. My mother's instructions at bedtime would be lacquered with mock-urgent tones. Or a word like *sí*, sounded in several notes, would convey added measures of feeling. Tongues lingered around the edges of words, especially fat vowels, and we happily sounded that military drum roll, the twirling roar of the Spanish *r*. Family language, my family's sounds: the voices of my parents and sisters and brother. Their voices insisting: *You belong here. We are family members. Related. Special to one another. Listen!* Voices singing and sighing, rising and straining, then surging, teeming with pleasure which burst syllables into fragments of laughter. At times it seemed there was steady quiet only when, from another room, the rustling whispers of my parents faded and I edged closer to sleep.

Supporters of bilingual education imply today that students like me miss a great deal by not being taught in their family's language. What they seem not to recognize is that, as a socially disadvantaged child, I regarded Spanish as a private language. It was a ghetto language that deepened and strengthened my feeling of public separateness. What I needed to learn in school was that I had the right, and the obligation, to speak the public language. The odd truth is that my first-grade classmates could have become bilingual, in the conventional sense of the word, more easily than I. Had they been taught early (as upper-middle-class children often are taught) a "second language" like Spanish or French, they could have regarded it simply as another public language. In my case, such bilingualism could not have been so quickly achieved. What I did not believe was that I could speak a single public language.

Without question, it would have pleased me to have heard my teachers address me in Spanish when I entered the classroom. I would have felt much less afraid. I would have imagined that my instructors were somehow "related" to me; I would indeed have heard their Spanish as my family's language. I would have trusted them and responded with ease. But I would have delayed—postponed for how long?—having to learn the language of public society. I would have evaded—and for how long?—learning the great lesson of school: that I had a public identity.

Fortunately, my teachers were unsentimental about their responsibility. What they understood was that I needed to speak public English. So their voices would search me out, asking me questions. Each time I heard them I'd look up in surprise to see a nun's face frowning at me. I'd mumble, not really meaning to answer. The nun would persist. "Richard, stand up. Don't look at the floor. Speak up. Speak to the entire class, not just to me!" But I couldn't believe English could be my language to use. (In part, I did not want to believe it.) I continued to mumble. I resisted the teacher's demands. (Did I somehow suspect that once I learned this public language my family life would be changed?) Silent, waiting for the bell to sound, I remained dazed, diffident, afraid.

Because I wrongly imagined that English was intrinsically a public language and Spanish was intrinsically private, I easily noted the difference between classroom language and the language at home. At school, words were directed to a general audience of listeners. ("Boys and girls . . .") Words were meaningfully ordered. And the point was not self-expression alone, but to make oneself understood by many others. The teacher quizzed: "Boys and girls, why do we use that word in this sentence? Could we think of a better word to use there? Would the sentence change its meaning if the words were differently arranged? Isn't there a better way of saying much the same thing?" (I couldn't say. I wouldn't try to say.)

Three months passed. Five. A half year. Unsmiling, ever watchful, my teachers noted my silence. They began to connect my behavior with the slow progress my brother and sisters were making. Until, one Saturday morning, three nuns arrived at the house to talk to our parents. Stiffly they sat on the blue livingroom sofa. From the doorway of another room, spying on the visitors, I noted the incongruity, the clash of two worlds, the faces and voices of school intruding upon the familiar setting of home. I overheard one voice gently wondering, "Do your children speak only in Spanish at home,

Mrs. Rodriguez?" While another voice added, "That Richard especially seems so timid and shy."

That Rich-heard!

With great tact, the visitors continued, "Is it possible for you and your husband to encourage your children to practice their English when they are home?" Of course my parents complied. What would they not do for their children's well-being? And how could they question the Church's authority which those women represented? In an instant they agreed to give up the language (the sounds) which had revealed and accentuated our family's closeness. The moment after the visitors left, the change was observed. "*Ahora,* speak to us only *en inglés,*" my father and mother told us.

At first, it seemed a kind of game. After dinner each night, the family gathered together to practice "our" English. It was still then *inglés*, a language foreign to us, so we felt drawn to it as strangers. Laughing, we would try to define words we could not pronounce. We played with strange English sounds, often over-anglicizing our pronunciations. And we filled the smiling gaps of our sentences with familiar Spanish sounds. But that was cheating, somebody shouted, and everyone laughed.

In school, meanwhile, like my brother and sisters, I was required to attend a daily tutoring session. I needed a full year of this special work. I also needed my teachers to keep my attention from straying in class by calling out "*Rich-heard*"—their English voices slowly loosening the ties to my other name, with its three notes, *Ri-car-do*. Most of all, I needed to hear my mother and father speak to me in a moment of seriousness in "broken"—suddenly heartbreaking—English. This scene was inevitable. One Saturday morning I entered the kitchen where my parents were talking, but I did not realize that they were talking in Spanish until, the moment they saw me, their voices changed and they began speaking English. The gringo sounds they uttered startled me. Pushed me away. In that moment of trivial misunderstanding and profound insight, I felt my throat twisted by unsounded grief. I simply turned and left the room. But I had no place to escape to where I could grieve in Spanish. My brother and sisters were speaking English in another part of the house.

Again and again in the days following, as I grew increasingly angry, I was obliged to hear my mother and father encouraging me: "Speak to us *en inglés*." Only then did I determine to learn classroom English. Thus, sometime afterward it happened: One day in school, I raised my hand to volunteer an answer to a question. I spoke out in a loud voice and I did not think it remarkable when the entire class understood. That day I moved very far from being the disadvantaged child I had been only days earlier. Taken hold at last was the belief, the calming assurance, that I *belonged* in public.

Shortly after, I stopped hearing the high, troubling sounds of *los gringos*. A more and more confident speaker of English, I didn't listen to how strangers sounded when they talked to me. With so many English-speaking people around me, I no longer heard American accents. Conversations quickened. Listening to persons whose voices sounded eccentrically pitched, I might note their sounds for a few seconds, but then I'd concentrate on what they were saying. Now when I heard someone's tone of voice—angry or questioning or sarcastic or happy or sad—I didn't distinguish it from the words it expressed. Sound and word were thus tightly wedded. At the end of each day I was often bemused, and always relieved, to realize how "soundless," though crowded with words, my day in public had been. An eight-year-old boy, I finally came to accept what had been technically true since my birth: I was an American citizen.

But diminished by then was the special feeling of closeness at home. Gone was the desperate, urgent, intense feeling of being at home among those with whom I felt intimate. Our family remained a loving family, but one greatly changed. We were no longer so close, no longer bound tightly together by the knowledge of our separateness from *los gringos*. Neither my older brother nor my sisters rushed home after school any more. Nor did I. When I arrived home, often there would be neighborhood kids in the house. Or the house would be empty of sounds.

Following the dramatic Americanization of their children, even my parents grew more publicly confident—especially my mother. First she learned the names of all the people on the block. Then she decided we needed to have a telephone in our house. My father, for his part, continued to use the word gringo, but it was no longer charged with bitterness or distrust. Stripped of any emotional content, the word simply became a name for those Americans not of Hispanic descent. Hearing him, sometimes, I wasn't sure if he was pronouncing the Spanish word *gringo*, or saying gringo in English.

There was a new silence at home. As we children learned more and more English, we shared fewer and fewer words with our parents. Sentences needed to be spoken slowly when one of us addressed our mother or father. Often the parent wouldn't understand. The child would need to repeat himself. Still the parent misunderstood. The young voice, frustrated, would end up saying, "Never mind"—the subject was closed. Dinners would be noisy with the clinking of knives and forks against dishes. My mother would smile softly between her remarks; my father, at the other end of the table, would chew and chew his food while he stared over the heads of his children.

My mother! My father! After English became my primary language, I no longer knew what words to use in addressing my parents. The old Spanish words (those tender accents of sound) I had earlier used—*mamá* and *papá*—I couldn't use any more. They would have been all-too-painful reminders of how much had changed in my life. On the other hand, the words I heard neighborhood kids call their parents seemed equally unsatisfactory. "Mother" and "father," "ma," "papa," "pa," "dad," "pop" (how I hated the all-American sound of that last word)—all these I felt were unsuitable terms of address for *my* parents. As a result, I never used them at home. Whenever I'd speak to my parents, I would try to get their attention by looking at them. In public conversations, I'd refer to them as my "parents" or my "mother" and "father."

My mother and father, for their part, responded differently, as their children spoke to them less. My mother grew restless, seemed troubled and anxious at the scarceness of words exchanged in the house. She would question me about my day when I came home from school. She smiled at my small talk. She pried at the edges of my sentences to get me to say something more ("What . . . ?") She'd join conversations she overheard, but her intrusions often stopped her children's talking. By contrast, my father seemed to grow reconciled to the new quiet. Though his English somewhat improved, he tended more and more to retire into silence. At dinner he spoke very little. One night his children and even his wife helplessly giggled at his garbled English pronunciation of the Catholic "Grace Before Meals." Thereafter he made his wife recite the prayer at the start of each meal, even on formal occasions when there were guests in the house.

Hers became the public voice of the family. On official business it was she, not my father, who would usually talk to strangers on the phone or in stores. We children grew so accustomed to his silence that years later we would routinely refer to his "shyness." (My mother often tried to explain: Both of his parents died when he was eight. He was raised by an uncle who treated him as little more than a menial servant. He was never encouraged to speak. He grew up alone—a man of few words.) But I realized my father was not shy whenever I'd watch him speaking Spanish with relatives. Using Spanish, he was quickly effusive. Especially when talking with other men, his voice would spark, flicker, flare alive with varied sounds. In Spanish he expressed ideas and feelings he rarely revealed when speaking English. With firm Spanish sounds he conveyed a confidence and authority that English would never allow him.

The silence at home, however, was not simply the result of fewer words passing between parents and children. More profound for me was the silence created by my inattention to sounds. At about the time I no longer bothered to listen with care to the sounds of English in public, I grew careless about listening to the sounds made by the family when they spoke. Most of the time I would hear someone speaking at home and didn't distinguish his sounds from the words people uttered in public. I didn't even pay much attention to my parents' accented and ungrammatical speech—at least not at home. Only when I was with them in public would I become alert to their accents. But even then their sounds caused me less and less concern. For I was growing increasingly confident of my own public identity.

I would have been happier about my public success had I not recalled, sometimes, what it had been like earlier, when my family conveyed its intimacy through a set of conveniently private sounds. Sometimes in public, hearing a stranger, I'd hark back to my lost past. A Mexican farm worker approached me one day downtown. He wanted directions to some place. "*Hijito,* . . ." he said. And his voice stirred old longings. Another time I was standing beside my mother in the visiting room of a Carmelite convent, before the dense screen which rendered the nuns shadowy figures. I heard several of them speaking Spanish in their busy, singsong, overlapping voices, assuring my mother that, yes, yes, we were remembered, all our family was remembered, in their prayers. Those voices echoed faraway family sounds. Another day a dark-faced old woman touched my shoulder lightly to steady herself as she boarded a bus. She murmured something to me I couldn't quite comprehend. Her Spanish voice came near, like the face of a never-before-seen relative in the instant before I was kissed. That voice, like so many of the Spanish voices I'd hear in public, recalled the golden age of my childhood.

Bilingual educators say today that children lose a degree of "individuality" by becoming assimilated into public society. (Bilingual schooling is a program popularized in the seventies, that decade when middle-class "ethnics" began to resist the process of assimilation—the "American melting pot.") But the bilingualists oversimplify when they scorn the value and necessity of assimilation. They do not seem to realize that a person is individualized in two ways. So they do not realize that, while one suffers a diminished sense of *private* individuality by being assimilated into public society, such assimilation makes possible the achievement of *public* individuality.

Simplistically again, the bilingualists insist that a student should be reminded of his difference from others in mass society, of his "heritage." But they equate mere separateness with individuality. The fact is that only in private—with intimates—is separateness from the crowd a prerequisite for individuality; an intimate "tells" me that I am unique, unlike all others, apart from the crowd. In public, by contrast, full individuality is achieved paradoxically, by those who are able to consider themselves members of the crowd. Thus it happened for me. Only when I was able to think of myself as an American, no longer an alien in gringo society, could I seek the rights and opportunities necessary for full public individuality. The social and political advantages I enjoy as a man began on the day I came to believe that my name is indeed *Rich-heard Road-ree-guess*. It is true that my public society today is often impersonal; in fact, my public society is usually mass society. But despite the anonymity of the crowd, and despite the fact that the individuality I achieve in public is often tenuous—because it depends on my being one in a crowd—I celebrate the day I acquired my new name. Those middle-class ethnics who scorn assimilation seem to me filled with decadent self-pity, obsessed by the burden of public life. Dangerously, they romanticize public separateness and trivialize the dilemma of those who are truly socially disadvantaged.

If I rehearse here the changes in my private life after my Americanization, it is finally to emphasize a public gain. The loss implies the gain. The house I returned to each afternoon was quiet. Intimate sounds no longer greeted me at the door. Inside there were other noises. The telephone rang. Neighborhood kids ran past the door of the bedroom where I was reading my schoolbooks—covered with brown shopping-bag paper. Once I learned the public language, it would never again be easy for me to hear intimate family voices. More and more of my day was spent hearing words, not sounds. But that may only be a way of saying that on the day I raised my hand in class and spoke loudly to an entire roomful of faces, my childhood started to end.

12

"Reading Has Always Been My Home," from *How Reading Changed My Life*

Anna Quindlen

*Quindlen shares her love of reading, both nonfiction
and fiction, which takes her away to other worlds.
She believes that our society does not truly value this
kind of reading, even though we may say that we do.
As a nation, it appears that we value reading for
advancement or reading that leads to a career, but not
reading for the sheer pleasure of it.*

Reading has always been my home, my sustenance, my great invincible companion. "Book love," Trollope called it. "It will make your hours pleasant to you as long as you live." Yet of all the many things in which we recognize some universal comfort—God, sex, food, family, friends—reading seems to be the one in which comfort is the most undersung, at least publicly, although it was really all I thought of, or felt, when I was eating up book after book, running away from home while sitting in that chair, traveling around the world and yet never leaving the room. I did not read from a sense of superiority, or advancement, or even learning. I read because I loved it more than any other activity on earth.

By the time I became an adult, I realized that while my satisfaction in the sheer act of reading had not abated in the least, the world was often as hostile, or at least as blind, to that joy as had been my girlfriends banging on our screen door, begging me to put down the book—"that stupid book," they usually called it, no matter what book it happened to be. While we pay lip service to the virtues of reading, the truth is that there is still in our culture something that suspects those who read too much, whatever reading too much means, of being lazy, aimless dreamers, people who need to grow up and come outside to where real life is, who think themselves superior in their separateness.

There is something in the American character that is even secretly hostile to the act of aimless reading, a certain hale and heartiness that is suspicious of reading as anything more than a tool for advancement. This is a country that likes confidence but despises hubris, that associates the "nose in the book" with a sense of covert superiority. America is also a nation that prizes sociability and community, that accepts a kind of psychological domino effect; alone leads to loner, loner to loser. Any sort of turning away from human contact is suspect, especially one that interferes with the go-out-and-get-going ethos that seems to be at the heart of our national character. The images of American presidents that stick are those that portray them as men of action: Theodore Roosevelt on safari, John Kennedy throwing a football around with his brothers. There is only Lincoln as solace to the inveterate reader, a solitary figure sitting by the fire, saying, "My best friend is a person who will give me a book I have not read."

There also arose, as I was growing up, a kind of careerism in the United States that sanctioned reading only if there was some point to it. Students at the nation's best liberal arts colleges who majored in philosophy or English were constantly asked what they were "going to do with it" as though intellectual pursuits for their own sake had had their day, and lost it in the press of business. Reading for pleasure was replaced by reading for purpose, and a kind of dogged self-improvement: whereas an executive might learn far more from *Moby Dick* or *The Man in the Grey Flannel Suit*, the book he was expected to have read might be *The Seven Habits of Highly*

Effective People. Reading for pleasure, spurred on by some interior compulsion, became as suspect as getting on the subway to ride aimlessly from place to place, or driving from nowhere to nowhere in a car. I like to do both those things, too, but not half so much as reading.

13

"Brownsville Schooldays," from *A Walker in the City*

Alfred Kazin

Kazin examines the lessons that immigrant children learn in school. He describes the humiliation of constant scrutiny by callous teachers, the struggle to speak a new language, and the saving grace of his private reading.

All my early life lies open to my eye within five city blocks. When I passed the school, I went sick with all my old fear of it. With its standard New York public-school brown brick courtyard shut in on three sides of the square and the pretentious battlements overlooking that cockpit in which I can still smell the fiery sheen of the rubber ball, it looks like a factory over which has been imposed the façade of a castle. It gave me the shivers to stand up in that courtyard again; I felt as if I had been mustered back into the service of those Friday morning "tests" that were the terror of my childhood.

It was never learning I associated with that school: only the necessity to succeed, to get ahead of the others in the daily struggle to "make a good impression" on our teachers, who grimly, wearily, and often with ill-concealed distaste watched against our relapsing into the natural savagery they expected of Brownsville boys. The white, cool, thinly ruled record book sat over us from their desks all day long, and had remorselessly entered into it each day—in blue ink if we had passed, in red ink if we had not—our attendance, our conduct, our "effort," our merits and demerits; and to the last possible decimal point in calculation, our standing in an unending series of "tests"—surprise tests, daily tests, weekly tests, formal midterm tests, final tests. They never stopped trying to dig out of us whatever small morsel of fact we had managed to get down the night before. We had to prove that we were really alert, ready for anything, always in the race. That white thinly ruled record book figured in my mind as the judgment seat; the very thinness and remote blue lightness of its lines instantly showed its cold authority over me; so much space had been left on each page, columns and columns in which to note down everything about us, implacably and forever. As it lay there on a teacher's desk, I stared at it all day long with such fear and anxious propriety that I had no trouble believing that God, too, did nothing but keep such record books, and that on the final day He would face me with an account in Hebrew letters whose phonetic dots and dashes looked strangely like decimal points counting up my every sinful thought on earth.

All teachers were to be respected like gods, and God Himself was the greatest of all school superintendents. Long after I had ceased to believe that our teachers could see with the back of their heads, it was still understood, by me, that they knew everything. They were the delegates of all visible and invisible power on earth—of the mothers who waited on the stoops every day after three for us to bring home tales of our daily triumphs; of the glacially remote Anglo-Saxon principal, whose very name was King; of the incalculably important Superintendent of Schools who would someday rubberstamp his name to the bottom of our diplomas in grim acknowledgment that we had, at last, given satisfaction to him, to the Board of Superintendents, and to our benefactor the City of New York—and so up and up, to the government of the United States and to the great Lord Jehovah Himself. My belief in teachers' unlimited wisdom and power rested not so much on what I saw in them—how impatient most of them looked, how wary—but on our abysmal humility, at least in those of us who were "good" boys, who proved by our ready compliance and "manners" that we wanted to get on. The road to a professional future would be shown us only as we pleased *them. Make a good impression the first day of the term, and they'll help you out. Make a bad impression, and you might as well cut your throat.* This was the first article of school folklore, whispered around the classroom the opening day of each term. You made the "good impression" by sitting firmly at your wooden desk, hands clasped; by silence for the greatest part of the live-long day; by standing up obsequiously when it was so expected of you; by sitting down noiselessly when you had answered a question; by "speaking nicely," which meant reproducing their painfully exact enunciation; by "showing manners," or an ecstatic submissiveness in all things; by outrageous flattery; by bringing little gifts at Christmas, on their birthdays, and at the end of the term—the well-known significance of these gifts being that they came not from us, but from our parents, whose eagerness in this matter showed a high level of social consideration, and thus raised our standing in turn.

It was not just our quickness and memory that were always being tested. Above all, in that word I could never hear without automatically seeing it raised before me in gold-plated letters, it was our *character.* I always felt anxious when I heard the word pronounced. Satisfactory as my "character" was, on the whole, except when I stayed too long in the playground reading; outrageously satisfactory, as I can see now, the very sound of the word as our teachers coldly gave it out from the end of their teeth, with a solemn weight on each dark syllable, immediately struck my heart cold with fear— they could not believe I really had it. Character was never something you had; it had to be trained in you, like a technique. I was never very clear about it. On our side *character* meant demonstrative obedience; but teachers already had it—how else could they have become teachers? They had it; the aloof Anglo-Saxon principal whom we remotely saw only on ceremonial occasions in the assembly was positively encased in it; it glittered off his bald head in spokes of triumphant light; the President of the United States had the greatest conceivable amount of it. Character belonged to great adults. Yet we were constantly being driven onto it; it was the great threshold we had to cross. *Alfred Kazin, having shown proficiency in his course of studies and having displayed satisfactory marks of character . . .* Thus someday the hallowed diploma, passport to my further advancement in high school. But there—I could already feel it in my bones—they would put me through even more doubting tests of character; and after that, if I should be good enough and bright enough, there would be still more. *Character* was a bitter thing, racked with my endless striving to please. The school—from every last stone in the courtyard to the battlements frowning down at me from the walls—was only the stage for a trial. I felt that the very atmosphere of learning that surrounded us was fake—that every lesson, every book, every approving smile was only a pretext for the constant probing and watching of me, that there was not a secret in me that would not be decimally measured into that white record book. All week long I lived for the blessed sound of the dismissal gong at three o'clock on Friday afternoon.

I was awed by this system, I believed in it, I respected its force. The alternative was "going bad." The school was notoriously the toughest in our tough neighborhood, and the dangers of "going bad" were constantly impressed upon me at home and in school in dark whispers of the "reform school" and in examples of boys who had been picked up for petty thievery, rape, or flinging a heavy inkwell straight into a teacher's face. Behind any failure in school yawned the great abyss of a criminal career. Every refractory attitude doomed you with the sound "Sing Sing."[1] Anything less than absolute perfection in school always suggested to my mind that I might fall out of the daily race, be kept back in the working class forever, or—dared I think of it?—fall into the criminal class itself.

I worked on a hairline between triumph and catastrophe. Why the odds should always have felt so narrow I understood only when

I realized how little my parents thought of their own lives. It was not for myself alone that I was expected to shine, but for them—to redeem the constant anxiety of their existence. I was the first American child, their offering to the strange new God; I was to be the monument of their liberation from the shame of being—what they were. And that there was shame in this was a fact that everyone seemed to believe as a matter of course. It was in the gleeful discounting of themselves—what do we know?—with which our parents greeted every fresh victory in our savage competition for "high averages," for prizes, for a few condescending words of official praise from the principal at assembly. It was in the sickening invocation of "Americanism"—the word itself accusing us of everything we apparently were not. Our families and teachers seemed tacitly agreed that we were somehow to be a little ashamed of what we were. Yet it was always hard to say why this should be so. It was certainly not—in Brownsville!—because we were Jews, or simply because we spoke another language at home, or were absent on our holy days. It was rather that a "refined," "correct," "nice" English was required of us at school that we did not naturally speak, and that our teachers could never be quite sure we would keep. This English was peculiarly the ladder of advancement. Every future young lawyer was known by it. Even the Communists and Socialists on Pitkin Avenue spoke it. It was bright and clean and polished. We were expected to show it off like a new pair of shoes. When the teacher sharply called a question out, then your name, you were expected to leap up, face the class, and eject those new words fluently off the tongue.

There was my secret ordeal: I could never say anything except in the most roundabout way; I was a stammerer. Although I knew all those new words from my private reading—I read walking in the street, to and from the Children's Library on Stone Avenue; on the fire escape and the roof; at every meal when they would let me; read even when I dressed in the morning, propping my book up against the drawers of the bureau as I pulled on my long black stockings—I could never seem to get the easiest words out with the right dispatch, and would often miserably signal from my desk that I did not know the answer rather than get up to stumble and fall and crash on every word. If, angry at always being put down as lazy or stupid, I did get up to speak, the black wooden floor would roll away under my feet, the teacher would frown at me in amazement, and in unbearable loneliness I would hear behind me the groans and laughter: *tuh-tuh-tuh-tuh*.

The word was my agony. The word that for others was so effortless and so neutral, so unburdened, so simple, so exact, I had first to meditate in advance, to see if I could make it, like a plumber fitting together odd lengths and shapes of pipe. I was always preparing words I could speak, storing them away, choosing between them. And often, when the word did come from my mouth as a great and terrible birth, quailing and bleeding as if forced through a thornbush, I would not be able to look the others in the face, and would walk out in the silence, the infinitely echoing silence behind my back, to say it all cleanly back to myself as I walked in the streets. Only when I was alone in the open air pacing the roof with pebbles in my mouth, as I had read Demosthenes had done to cure himself of stammering; or in the street, where all words seemed to flow from the length of my stride and the color of the houses as I remembered the perfect tranquillity of a phrase in Beethoven's *Romance in F* I could sing back to myself as I walked—only then was it possible for me to speak without the infinite premeditations and strangled silences I toiled through whenever I got up at school to respond with the expected, the exact answer.

It troubled me that I could speak in the fullness of my own voice only when I was alone on the streets, walking about. There was something unnatural about it; unbearably isolated. I was not like the others! I was not like the others! At midday, every freshly shocking Monday noon, they sent me away to a speech clinic in a school in East New York, where I sat in a circle of lispers and cleft palates and foreign accents holding a mirror before my lips and rolling difficult sounds over and over. To be sent there in the full light of the opening week, when everyone else was at school or going about his business, made me feel as if I had been expelled from the great normal body of humanity. I would gobble down my lunch on my way to the speech clinic and rush back to the school in time to make up for the classes I had lost. One day, one unforgettable dread day, I stopped to catch my breath on a corner of Sutter Avenue, near the wholesale fruit markets, where an old drugstore rose up over a great flight of steps. In the window were dusty urns of colored water floating off iron chains; cardboard placards advertising hairnets, Ex-Lax; a great illustrated medical chart headed THE HUMAN FACTORY, which showed the exact course a mouthful of food follows as it falls from chamber to chamber of the body. I hadn't meant to stop there at all, only to catch my breath; but I so hated the speech clinic that I thought I would delay my arrival for a few minutes by eating my lunch on the steps. When I took the sandwich out of my bag, two bitterly hard pieces of hard salami slipped out of my hand and fell through a grate onto a hill of dust below the steps. I remember how sickeningly vivid an odd thread of hair looked on the salami, as if my lunch were turning stiff with death. The factory whistles called their short, sharp blasts stark through the middle of noon, beating at me where I sat outside the city's magnetic circle. I had never known, I knew instantly I would never in my heart again submit to, such wild passive despair as I felt at that moment, sitting on the steps before THE HUMAN FACTORY, where little robots gathered and shoveled the food from chamber to chamber of the body. They had put me out into the streets, I thought to myself; with their mirrors and their everlasting pulling at me to imitate their effortless bright speech and their stupefaction that a boy could stammer and stumble on every other English word he carried in his head, they had put me out into the streets, had left me high and dry on the steps of that drugstore staring at the remains of my lunch turning black and grimy in the dust.

In the great cool assembly hall, dominated by the gold sign above the stage, KNOWLEDGE IS POWER, the windowsills were lined with Dutch bulbs, each wedged into a mound of pebbles massed in a stone dish. Above them hung a giant photograph of Theodore Roosevelt. Whenever I walked in to see the empty assembly hall for myself, the shiny waxed floor of the stage dangled in the middle of the air like a crescent. On one side was a great silk American flag, the staff crowned by a gilt eagle. Across the dry rattling of varnish-smelling empty seats bowing to the American flag, I saw in the play of the sun on those pebbles wildly sudden images of peace. *There* was the other land, crowned by the severe and questioning face of Theodore Roosevelt, his eyes above the curiously endearing straw-dry mustache, behind the pince-nez glittering with light, staring and staring me through as if he were uncertain whether he fully approved of me.

The light pouring through window after window in that great empty varnished assembly hall seemed to me the most wonderful thing I had ever seen. It was that thorough varnished cleanness that was of the new land, that light dancing off the glasses of Theodore Roosevelt, those green and white roots of the still raw onion-brown bulbs delicately flaring up from the hill of pebbles into which they were wedged. The pebbles moved me in themselves, there were so many of them. They rose up around the bulbs in delicately strong masses of colored stone, and as the sun fell between them, each pebble shone in its own light. Looking across the great rows of empty seats to those pebbles lining the windowsills, I could still smell summer from some long veranda surrounded by trees. On that veranda sat the family and friends of Theodore Roosevelt. I knew the name: Oyster Bay. Because of that picture, I had read *The Boy's Life of Theodore Roosevelt*; knew he had walked New York streets night after night as Police Commissioner, unafraid of the Tenderloin gangsters; had looked into *Theodore Roosevelt's Letters to His Children*, pretending that those hilarious drawings on almost every page were for me. *There* was America, I thought, the real America, *his* America, where from behind the glass on the wall of our assembly hall he watched over us to make sure we did right, thought right, lived right.

"Up, boys! Up San Juan Hill!" I still hear our roguish old civics teacher, a little white-haired Irishman who was supposed to have been with Teddy in Cuba, driving us through our Friday morning tests with these shouts and cries. He called them "Army Navy" tests, to make us feel big, and dividing the class between Army and Navy, got us to compete with each other for a coveted blue star. Civics was city government, state government, federal government; each government had functions; you had to get them out fast in order to win for the Army or the Navy. Sometimes this required filling in three or four words, line by line, down one side of the grimly official yellow foolscap that was brought out for tests. (In the tense silence just before the test began, he looked at us sharply, the watch in his hand ticking as violently as the sound of my heart, and on command, fifty boys simultaneously folded their yellow test paper and evened the fold with their thumbnails in a single dry sigh down the middle of the paper.) At other times it meant true-or-false tests; then he stood behind us to make sure we did not signal the right answers to each other in the usual way—for true, nodding your head; for false, holding your nose. You could hear his voice barking from the rear. "*Come on now, you Army boys! On your toes like West Point cadets! All ready now? Get set! Go! Three powers of the legislative branch? The judiciary? The executive? The subject of the fifteenth amendment? The capital of Wyoming? Come on, Navy! Shoot those landlubbers down! Give 'em a blast from your big guns right through the middle! The third article of the Bill of Rights? The thirteenth amendment? The sixteenth? True or false, Philadelphia is the capital of Pennsylvania. Up and at 'em, Navy! Mow them down! COME ON!!!*" Our "average" was calculated each week, and the boys who scored 90 percent or over were rewarded by seeing *their own names* lettered on the great blue chart over the blackboard. Each time I entered that room for a test, I looked for my name on the blue chart as if the sight of it would decide my happiness for all time.

Down we go, down the school corridors of the past smelling of chalk, lysol out of the open toilets, and girl sweat. The staircases were a gray stone I saw nowhere else in the school, and they were shut in on both sides by some thick unreflecting glass on which were pasted travel posters inviting us to spend the summer in the Black Forest. Those staircases created a spell in me that I had found my way to some distant, cool, neutral passageway deep in the body of the school. There, enclosed within the thick, green boughs of a classic summer in Germany, I could still smell the tense probing chalk smells from every classroom, the tickling high surgical odor of lysol from the open toilets, could still hear that continuous babble, babble of water dripping into the bowls. Sex was instantly connected in my mind with the cruel openness of those toilets, and in the never-ending sound of the bowls being flushed I could detect, as I did in the maddeningly elusive fragrance of cologne brought into the classroom by Mrs. B., the imminence of something severe, frightening, obscene. Sex, as they said in the "Coney Island" dives outside the school, was like going to the toilet; there was a great contempt in this that made me think of the wet rings left by our sneakers as we ran down the gray stone steps after school.

Outside the women teachers' washroom on the third floor, the tough guys would wait for the possible appearance of Mrs. B., whose large goiterous eyes seemed to bulge wearily with mischief, who always looked tired and cynical, and who wore thin chiffon dresses that affected us much more than she seemed to realize. Mrs. B. often went about the corridors in the company of a trim little teacher of mathematics who was a head shorter than she and had a mustache. Her chiffon dresses billowed around him like a sail; she seemed to have him in tow. It was understood by us as a matter of course that she wore those dresses to inflame us; that she *was* tired and cynical, from much practice in obscene lovemaking; that she was a "bad one" like the young Polish blondes from East New York I occasionally saw in the "Coney Island" dives sitting on someone's lap and smoking a cigarette. How wonderful and unbelievable it was to find this in a teacher; to realize that the two of them, after we had left the school, probably met to rub up against each other in the faculty toilet. Sex was a grim test where sooner or later you would have to prove yourself doing things to women. In the smell of chalk and sweat and the unending smirky babble of the water as it came to me on the staircase through my summer's dream of old Germany, I could feel myself being called to still another duty—to conquer Mrs. B., to rise to the challenge she had whispered to us in her sly-ness. I had seen pictures of it on the block—they were always pass-ing them around between handball games—the man's face furious, ecstatic with lewdness as he proudly looked down at himself; the woman sniggering as she teased him with droplets from the contra-ceptive someone had just shown me in the gutter—its crushed, filmy slyness the very sign of the forbidden.

They had never said anything about this at home, and I thought I knew why. Sex was the opposite of books, of pictures, of music, of the open air, even of kindness. They would not let you have both. Something always lingered to the sound of those toilets to test you. In and out of the classroom they were always testing you. *Come on, Army! Come on, Navy!* As I stood up in that school courtyard and smelled again the familiar sweat, heard again the unending babble from the open toilets, I suddenly remembered how sure I had always been that even my failures in there would be entered in a white, thinly ruled, official record book.

Note

1. Sing Sing was a New York State prison known for its brutal treat-ment of prisoners.

Part II

Literacy and Power

Selections show how reading and writing open doors in our lives.

"Gary Lee," from *Speaking of Reading*

Gary Lee

"The world is set up to where you've got to read and write to be able to function in it. It's really frustrating if you can't, and you beat up on yourself a lot," says Lee, who is learning how to read, fifteen years after receiving his high school diploma. He and two other students from his adult literacy class have written and produced a play that dramatizes the frustrations and limitations of a life without literacy.

Schools are big factories. When you're a little kid, you're the raw material, and when you get to the end, they spit you out. Somewhere in between, if you don't keep up, you get chucked off into the reject pile. That's basically what happened to me.

Reading has been a problem with me ever since I was a little kid. I went to three or four elementary schools. Before I even got to junior high, they put me into a special ed. class and that was what I would call the reject pile.

My mom and dad got a divorce when I was what? Seven years old? My mom was a waitress and was trying to raise two kids. She could read pretty good, but she wasn't a very advanced reader or anything. I went through a couple junior high schools and then I went to two different high schools. I guess I just got lost in the changes.

My mom, she never really stressed to me to go to school and learn stuff. She just said, "Go to school." So I went to school. But when I was in high school, the teachers would never make me do anything. I would go to class and they would say, "Well, you showed up, I'll give you a 'D.'" So I would go to school, but it was basically a big joke.

One teacher was real nice to me and helped me out, but then I moved again. I had to meet new friends, a whole new set of teachers. I guess some people don't realize that moving around really hurts a kid. As soon as you settle down and get used to the new set of teachers and friends, your family moves and you don't have any control over it.

One time in the shuffle, they got my papers screwed up and they injected me into a regular high school format. I went up to this one teacher and told her, "I can't read. I can't do this." They put me into the special ed. class, where we played cards. For two years. But they gave me a high school diploma at the end. Yeah, it's not worth the ink it's printed on. I didn't even care when I got it. I could have left school in the sixth grade.

No one in school ever tried to figure out what I was really talented at. The only thing they spent a lot of time figuring out was what I *wasn't* talented at. Nobody cared what I was interested in. Nobody ever tried to figure out what I could do and try to build off of that.

In the fifteen or so years since high school, I haven't done much. I like going to car races and I guess that's why I started learning to read. I read a lot of car magazines, although when I first started reading them, I was lousy at it. I would just sit down and try to read them as best I could. The words are fairly simple. Those were the only kind of magazines I would read because it was something I was interested in—I wanted to learn about the racing cars.

Then a couple of years ago I went to the literacy program because I was mad at myself. I was still running from this reading thing. I wanted to progress in my life and I knew I had to learn to read and write to do it. I looked in the front of the *Yellow Pages* where there's a lot of community services listed. The first time I went to the literacy program, it felt like I was going to the dentist. I didn't know what to expect. They gave me a couple tests and then they gave me a tutor. They don't have a magical wand or anything. They couldn't just crack me in the head and make me able to read and write.

I had one tutor for a couple of years, but then she went on to something different, I guess. Now I've got another one and she's very organized. She even makes me more organized because she makes me put down what time I study and what I study at what time. I like that. She tutors me for three hours and then she gives me six hours of homework. It really doesn't make my social life too great, but I do most of it anyway. The harder that I push, the farther I go. I don't want to be doing this for eight years.

I came up with this idea that I wanted to write a play about what it was like to not read and write. It's funny because I had never, ever been to a play, and I've never attempted to write one, and I've never attempted acting. It just popped into my head one day. I got together with two other students who were willing to go out on a limb with me. So we sat down and worked for about a year discussing our own personal trials on reading and what we could say out of it all. We sat down and wrote it and produced it and did most of the work ourselves.

We acted out parts of our three stories. My story was about when I got pulled from a regular school and got bussed around town to a special ed. class where the teacher was totally mean to me. She would always grab a hold of my ear and yank on it if I wasn't doing stuff right, or if she was frustrated at me or just was having a bad day. The second scene was about when one of the other students was in high school. I played the teacher and he played himself. The teacher tried to make him stand up in class and read, but he couldn't read and we showed the frustration in that. And the third scene is about when the third student is in high school and she goes to a counselor and he tells her that she doesn't have the ability to even learn how to read.

The play goes from grade school to high school and the very last scene is where the other male student goes to get a job and he can't fill out the application or run a computer because he doesn't know how to read so he's turned down for the job. We're putting the play on all around the area. There's a part in the play that goes something like, "I'm bound by invisible chains, but one of these days, I'm going to get rid of these chains that have bound me." People walk away from the play real sad. I guess that's what we wanted them to do, but I was surprised when I saw some people in the audience crying. But we make them laugh, too.

I used to think that I couldn't do anything, but now I think things are open to me pretty much. Believing in myself is a lot of it. In school all they taught me was, "You're not going to amount to anything. You're lousy at this, and you will always be lousy." Now I know I ain't the greatest, but if I work hard, I will overcome all of this. I want to be the first one in my family to learn to read and write to a high level. Then I want to go back to school and open my own business.

I know it's going to be a long haul. Learning to read takes time. But over time you get more familiar with it and it starts to become easier for you. It's like the first time I went skiing. I was falling all over the place. I was the lousiest skier in the world. But now that I've done it for a few years, I've gotten pretty good at it. The first time I went skiing, there was a tiny hump and I couldn't get up over it. Now a little hump like that would be nothing to me.

"Two Ways to Be a Warrior," from *Luis Rodriguez: Writer, Community Leader, Political Activist*

Michael Schwartz

Luis Rodriguez is a writer who travels the country speaking in schools about his troubled youth. He shares with students his discovery that words can be powerful tools for saving one's self. Upon finding his own powerful voice, he wrote his autobiography, Always Running, so that others would learn from his mistakes.

A ninth grader nervously raised her hand to ask a question in the school auditorium. "What do you do when you are worried about someone close to you who . . . ?" Her voice choked with emotion as she began to cry, and all heads in the auditorium turned.

"Is someone you know getting into this life?" Luis J. Rodriguez asked the girl.

She nodded. Luis looked at her for a few moments, then nodded his head in response. He seemed to understand the girl's feelings.

Luis J. Rodriguez had come to inner-city Hartford High School on this day to talk about his life. Twenty years earlier, he had been a member of a gang in East Los Angeles. He had hurt people, been shot at, been addicted to drugs, and had served time in jail. He and his friends had a special name for their experiences. They called it *La Vida Loca*—"the crazy life." By the time Luis was 18 years old, 25 of his friends had died due to violence. Somehow Luis not only survived *La Vida Loca* but also found a way to make a difference in the lives of others as a widely praised writer, journalist, and speaker.

"What you are talking about is very difficult," he told the girl in the auditorium. "The important thing is for you to try to be there for your friend. Try to understand what they are going through. Don't abandon them. If you can, keep them surrounded with friends and family, and don't give up on them."

Luis Rodriguez knows firsthand the dangers young people face in gangs. He knows he was lucky, but also believes that what saved him was finding something worthwhile in himself—something worth living for. He discovered that words were powerful tools that he could use to help himself and others. He realized there was a powerful voice inside him. Because of the power of words, Luis grew up to have a family and become a writer. He has been a factory worker as well as a newspaper reporter, an award-winning poet, a journalist, and a publisher.

However, as Luis entered his mid-30s, he saw his teenage son, Ramiro, having trouble at school, getting into fights, and facing pressures to join a neighborhood gang. It made Luis sad to see his son going through the dangers and difficulties that he had only barely managed to escape himself. Ramiro's problems made Luis feel a deep concern, not only for his son but for all young people growing up surrounded by gangs, drug addiction, and violence.

Luis decided to write the story of his life, the bad and the good, in order to share his experience with his son. He hoped Ramiro could avoid some of the mistakes that he had made.

He also wanted readers to understand and care about what is happening to many young people in cities and small towns today. He wanted to explain that young people involved in gangs are not monsters but rather human beings with problems.

Luis titled his book *Always Running*. The many years he had spent working on poetry and learning the craft of writing paid off. Educators and critics wrote to newspapers explaining how they felt Luis's story was truthful, influential, and written with the skill and power of an artist. Before *Always Running,* very few people had written so authentically about the lives of gang members.

With the success of *Always Running,* Luis appeared on national television and radio programs and was invited to travel across the country and even to Europe. In almost every city he went to, however, he also spent time visiting and talking with kids in youth groups, community centers, and schools, such as Hartford High School. He wanted to reach kids in trouble and to be an example of an older person who had faced and survived the same problems they were facing.

"If you saw me 20 years ago," he told the students at Hartford High School, "you wouldn't like me, and you'd probably stay away. I never said nothing to no one. I was cool, I was hard, I was tough, and I was very angry. I thought of myself as a kind of warrior. I didn't care if I died or who I brought down with me.

"When I almost died, it made me see things differently. I had an older friend who told me that there are two ways to be a warrior— to be a destroyer and die like one, or to create and live like one.

"The way to live like a warrior is to find the things that are important to you—in my case it was expression and writing—and dedicate your life to it. That's what I decided to do, and that's what kept me alive."

Luis told a reporter that when he visits schools and community centers, he prefers to have a conversation with kids rather than make a speech to them. At Hartford High School, he encouraged students to ask him questions. One boy asked, "What was it like to be in jail?"

"It was terrible," Luis said. "The worst part was that it felt like I lost whatever little bit of control I thought I had. In jail you can't choose anything—when you eat, what you eat, when you watch TV, or who you talk to. It was probably the hardest time of my life."

Another boy asked, "Why did you let your son join a gang?"

"You're asking a very hard question," Luis replied. "No father would let his son be in a gang, but it isn't a father's choice. Can a father really stop a son from doing anything? A father can listen, understand, give advice, give help, but he can't live his son's life for him. My son has to make his own way, make his own decisions, like I had to make mine. The best I can do is share what I know, respect him, and be there. He's old enough now."

Another student asked, "How did you get to be a writer? Were you always good at it?"

"No. It never came easy for me. I struggled a lot with language. We spoke Spanish at home but weren't allowed to use it in school. I started school without knowing any English, and got put in the back of the classroom and forgotten. So my Spanish and my English were both bad. I never thought in a million years that I would win literary awards or become a publisher or do any of the things I do. It's a very interesting story how I grew up and ended up here today."

"The Poets in the Kitchen," from *Reena and Other Stories*

Paule Marshall

*Marshall, an avid young reader, shares her joy at dis-
covering the voices of black writers at her local
library. The poems of Paul Dunbar connect so vividly
to her own life experiences that she begins searching
for more stories and books about "her people." Someday, she thinks, she may try to write herself.*

By the time I was eight or nine, I graduated from the corner of
the kitchen to the neighborhood library, and thus from the spoken to the written word. The Macon Street Branch of the Brook-
lyn Public Library was an imposing half block long edifice of heavy
gray masonry, with glass-paneled doors at the front and two tall
metal torches symbolizing the light that comes of learning flanking
the wide steps.

The inside was just as impressive. More steps—of pale marble with
gleaming brass railings at the center and sides—led up to the circulation desk, and a great pendulum clock gazed down from the bal-
cony stacks that faced the entrance. Usually stationed at the top of
the steps like the guards outside Buckingham Palace was the custo-
dian, a stern-faced West Indian type who for years, until I was old
enough to obtain an adult card, would immediately shoo me with
one hand into the Children's Room and with the other threaten me
into silence, a finger to his lips. You would have thought he was the

chief librarian and not just someone whose job it was to keep the brass polished and the clock wound. I put him in a story called "Barbados" years later and had terrible things happen to him at the end.

I was sheltered from the storm of adolescence in the Macon Street library, reading voraciously, indiscriminately, everything from Jane Austen to Zane Grey, but with a special passion for the long, full-blown, richly detailed eighteenth- and nineteenth-century picaresque tales: *Tom Jones, Great Expectations, Vanity Fair.*

But although I loved nearly everything I read and would enter full into the lives of the characters—indeed, would cease being myself and become them—I sensed a lack after a time. Something I couldn't quite define was missing. And then one day, browsing in the poetry section, I came across a book by someone called Paul Laurence Dunbar, and opening it, I found the photograph of a wistful, sad-eyed poet who to my surprise was black. I turned to a poem at random. "Little brown-baby wif spa'klin'/eyes/Come to yo' pappy an' set on his knee." Although I had a little difficulty at first with the words in dialect, the poem spoke to me as nothing I had read before of the closeness, the special relationship I had had with my father, who by then had become an ardent believer in Father Divine and gone to live in Father's "kingdom" in Harlem. Reading it helped to ease somewhat the tight knot of sorrow and longing I carried around in my chest that refused to go away. I read another poem: "Lias! Lias! Bless de Lawd!/Don' you know de day's/erbroad?/ Ef you don' get up, you scamp/Dey'll be trouble in dis camp." I laughed. It reminded me of the way my mother sometimes yelled at my sister and me to get out of bed in the mornings.

And another: "Seen my lady home las' night/Jump back, honey, jump back./Hel' huh han' an' sque'z it tight . . ." About love between a black man and a black woman. I had never seen that written about before and it roused in me all kinds of delicious feelings and hopes.

And I began to search then for books and stories and poems about "The Race" (as it was put back then), about my people. While not abandoning Thackeray, Fielding, Dickens and the others, I started asking the reference librarian, who was white, for books by Negro writers, although I must admit I did so at first with a feeling of shame—the shame I and many others used to experience in those days whenever the word "Negro" or "colored" came up.

No grade school literature student of mine had ever mentioned Dunbar or James Weldon Johnson or Langston Hughes. I didn't know that Zora Neale Hurston existed and was busy writing and being published during those years. Nor was I made aware of people like Frederick Douglass and Harriet Tubman—their spirit and example—or the great nineteenth-century abolitionist and feminist Sojourner Truth. There wasn't even Negro History Week when I attended P.S. 35 on Decatur Street!

. . . It was around that time also that I began harboring the dangerous thought of someday trying to write myself. Perhaps a poem about an apple tree, although I had never seen one. Or the story of a girl who could magically transplant herself to wherever she wanted to be in the world—such as Father Divine's kingdom in Harlem. Dunbar—his dark, eloquent face, his large volume of poems—permitted me to dream that I might someday write, and with something of the power with words my mother and her friends possessed.

17

"Libraries and the Attack on Illiteracy"

Timothy S. Healy

Healy proposes a larger role for libraries in eliminating illiteracy in America's large cities. With increased public will and financial commitment, he says, libraries can help individuals reach their potential, which will lead to a better life for everyone.

A growing problem in all America's large cities is the illiteracy of so many of their citizens. New York City has an estimated 1.5 million people over the age of sixteen who cannot read a newspaper or the instructions on a bottle of medicine. For these adults such simple tasks mean defeat, shame, and confusion. The consequences of illiteracy—unemployment or underemployment, social ostracism, the feeling of failure as a parent—all have one thing in common: the fear of being discovered.

Most programs to help such people are based on schools, but local public libraries have an edge. Adults can come to them without embarrassment and work in areas not furnished for children. In addition, libraries can do what schools seldom can: tailor literacy training to the immediate needs and interests of the learners. Their goals can be as different as reading bedtime stories, improving job skills, getting a driver's license, or simply filling out the innumerable forms for public assistance that are so much a part of the life of the poor.

The three New York Library systems have a total of 200 branches located in every part of the city, including many in its poorest areas. The New York Public Library, for example, runs eight literacy programs involving 1,000 students, some 50 teachers, and 200 volunteers. That effort, however, is dogged by money constraints, and each of our eight centers turns away at least as many people as it is able to accept.

The political leaders of our great cities could easily mobilize their libraries in a concerted attack on illiteracy. For instance, in New York City, if each of the 200 branches dealt with 200 learners, these libraries would reach 40,000 people each year. Experience shows that once the libraries have set a pattern other local institutions will follow their example, borrow their people, and extend their work even further.

It is easy to create a stereotype of people who are illiterate. They are by no means all unemployed; many in New York hold jobs; their intelligence and insights are those of mature and experienced adults. Volunteer teachers find them rewarding to work with and are enthusiastic about the progress many make.

The reward for the city is enormous expansion of human potential. A literacy center in the Bronx publishes an anthology of writings by its students; one of them tells how the classes he has attended "are helping people like me not just to read but to feel good about themselves." Libraries know that one of their principal tasks is the enablement of citizens. In each of our great cities, that enablement lies ready to hand, if only we have the urban will and the budget commitment to make it work.

18

"Learning to Read," from
The Autobiography of Malcolm X

Malcolm X, Alex Haley

*Malcolm X describes in his autobiography how read-
ing changed the course of his life: "As I see it today,
the ability to read awoke inside me some long dormant
craving to be mentally alive." He argues that the history of white people has perpetrated a fraud designed
to "hide the black man's true role in history."*

Many who today hear me somewhere in person, or on television, or those who read something I've said, will think I
went to school far beyond the eighth grade. This impression is due
entirely to my prison studies.

It had really begun back in the Charlestown Prison, when Bimbi
first made me feel envy of his stock of knowledge. Bimbi had always
taken charge of any conversation he was in, and I had tried to emu-
late him. But every book I picked up had few sentences which didn't
contain anywhere from one to nearly all of the words that might as
well have been in Chinese. When I just skipped those words, of
course, I really ended up with little idea of what the book said. So
I had come to the Norfolk Prison Colony still going through only
book-reading motions. Pretty soon, I would have quit even these
motions, unless I had received the motivation that I did.

I saw that the best thing I could do was get hold of a dictionary—
to study, to learn some words. I was lucky enough to reason also that

I should try to improve my penmanship. It was sad. I couldn't even write in a straight line. It was both ideas together that moved me to request a dictionary along with some tablets and pencils from the Norfolk Prison Colony school.

I spent two days just riffling uncertainly through the dictionary's pages. I'd never realized so many words existed! I didn't know *which* words I needed to learn. Finally, just to start some kind of action, I began copying.

In my slow, painstaking, ragged handwriting, I copied into my tablet everything printed on that first page, down to the punctuation marks.

I believe it took me a day. Then, aloud, I read back, to myself, everything I'd written on the tablet. Over and over, aloud, to myself, I read my own handwriting.

I woke up the next morning, thinking about those words—immensely proud to realize that not only had I written so much at one time, but I'd written words that I never knew were in the world. Moreover, with a little effort, I also could remember what many of these words meant. I reviewed the words whose meanings I didn't remember. Funny thing, from the dictionary first page right now, that "aardvark" springs to my mind. The dictionary had a picture of it, a long-tailed, long-eared, burrowing African mammal, which lives off termites caught by sticking out its tongue as an anteater does for ants.

I was so fascinated that I went on—I copied the dictionary's next page. And the same experience came when I studied that. With every succeeding page, I also learned of people and places and events from history. Actually the dictionary is like a miniature encyclopedia. Finally the dictionary's A section had filled a whole tablet—and I went on into the B's. That was the way I started copying what eventually became the entire dictionary. It went a lot faster after so much practice helped me to pick up handwriting speed. Between what I wrote in my tablet, and writing letters, during the rest of my time in prison I would guess I wrote a million words.

I suppose it was inevitable that as my word-base broadened, I could for the first time pick up a book and read and now begin to understand what the book was saying. Anyone who has read a great deal can imagine the new world that opened. Let me tell you something: from then until I left that prison in every free moment I had, if I was not reading in the library, I was reading on my bunk. You couldn't have gotten me out of books with a wedge. Between Mr. Muhammad's teachings, my correspondence, my visitors—usually Ella and Reginald—and my reading of books, months passed without me even thinking about being imprisoned. In fact, up to then, I never had been so truly free in my life.

The Norfolk Prison Colony's library was in the school building. A variety of classes was taught there by instructors who came from such places as Harvard and Boston universities. The weekly debates between inmate teams were also held in the school building. You would be astonished to know how worked up convict debaters and audiences would get over subjects like "Should Babies Be Fed Milk?"

Available on the prison library's shelves were books on just about every general subject. Much of the big private collection that Parkhurst had willed to the prison was still in crates and boxes in the back of the library—thousands of old books. Some of them looked ancient: covers faded, old-time parchment-looking binding. Parkhurst, I've mentioned, seemed to have been principally interested in history and religion. He had the money and the special interest to have a lot of books that you wouldn't have in general circulation. Any college library would have been lucky to get that collection.

As you can imagine, especially in a prison where there was heavy emphasis on rehabilitation, an inmate was smiled upon if he demonstrated an unusually intense interest in books. There was a sizable number of well-read inmates, especially the popular debaters. Some were said by many to be practically walking encyclopedias. They were almost celebrities. No university would ask any student to devour literature as I did when this new world opened to me, of being able to read and *understand*.

I read more in my room than in the library itself. An inmate who was known to read a lot could check out more than the permitted maximum number of books. I preferred reading in the total isolation of my own room.

When I had progressed to really serious reading, every night at about ten P.M. I would be outraged with the "lights out." It always seemed to catch me right in the middle of something engrossing.

Fortunately, right outside my door was a corridor light that cast a glow into my room. The glow was enough to read by, once my eyes adjusted to it. So when "lights out" came, I would sit on the floor where I could continue reading in that glow.

At one-hour intervals the night guards paced past every room. Each time I heard the approaching footsteps, I jumped into bed and feigned sleep. And as soon as the guard passed, I got back out of bed onto the floor area of that light-glow, where I would read for another fifty-eight minutes—until the guard approached again. That went on until three or four every morning. Three or four hours of sleep a night was enough for me. Often in the years in the streets I had slept less than that.

Mr. Muhammad, to whom I was writing daily, had no idea of what a new world had opened up to me through my efforts to document his teachings in books.

When I discovered philosophy, I tried to touch all the landmarks of philosophical development. Gradually, I read most of the old philosophers, Occidental and Oriental. The Oriental philosophers were the ones I came to prefer; finally, my impression was that most Occidental philosophy had largely been borrowed from the Oriental thinkers. Socrates, for instance, traveled in Egypt. Some sources even say that Socrates was initiated into some of the Egyptian mysteries. Obviously Socrates got some of his wisdom among the East's wise men.

I have often reflected upon the new vistas that reading opened to me. I knew right there in prison that reading had changed forever the course of my life. As I see it today, the ability to read awoke inside me some long dormant craving to be mentally alive. I certainly wasn't seeking any degree, the way a college confers a status symbol upon its students. My homemade education gave me, with every additional book that I read, a little bit more sensitivity to the deafness, dumbness, and blindness that was afflicting the black race in America. Not long ago, an English writer telephoned me from London, asking questions. One was, "What's your alma mater?" I told him, "Books." You will never catch me with a free fifteen minutes in which I'm not studying something I feel might be able to help the black man.

Yesterday I spoke in London, and both ways on the plane across the Atlantic I was studying a document about how the United Nations proposes to insure the human rights of the oppressed minorities of the world. The American black man is the world's most shameful case of minority oppression. What makes the black man think of himself as only an internal United States issue is just a catch-phrase, two words, "civil rights." How is the black man going to get "civil rights" before first he wins his *human* rights? If the American black man will start thinking about his *human* rights, and then start thinking of himself as part of one of the world's great peoples, he will see he has a case for the United Nations.

I can't think of a better case! Four hundred years of black blood and sweat invested here in America, and the white man still has the black man begging for what every immigrant fresh off the ship can take for granted the minute he walks down the gangplank.

But I'm digressing. I told the Englishman that my alma mater was books, a good library. Every time I catch a plane, I have with me a book that I want to read—and that's a lot of books these days. If I weren't out here every day battling the white man, I could spend the rest of my life reading, just satisfying my curiosity—because you can hardly mention anything I'm not curious about. I don't think anybody ever got more out of going to prison than I did. In fact, prison enabled me to study far more intensively than I would have if my life had gone differently and I had attended some college. I imagine that one of the biggest troubles with colleges is there are too many distractions, too much panty-raiding, fraternities, and boola-boola and all of that. Where else but in a prison could I have attacked my ignorance by being able to study intensely sometimes as much as fifteen hours a day?

Schopenhauer, Kant, Nietzsche, naturally, I read all of those. I don't respect them; I am just trying to remember some of those whose theories I soaked up in those years. These three, it's said, laid the groundwork on which the Fascist and Nazi philosophy was built. I don't respect them because it seems to me that most of their time was spent arguing about things that are not really important. They remind me of so many of the Negro "intellectuals," so-called, with whom I have come in contact—they are always arguing about something useless.

Spinoza impressed me for a while when I found out that he was black. A black Spanish Jew. The Jews excommunicated him because he advocated a pantheistic doctrine, something like the "allness of God," or "God in everything." The Jews read their burial services for Spinoza, meaning that he was dead as far as they were concerned; his family was run out of Spain, they ended up in Holland, I think.

I'll tell you something. The whole stream of Western philosophy has now wound up in a cul-de-sac. The white man has perpetrated upon himself, as well as upon the black man, so gigantic a fraud that he has put himself into a crack. He did it through his elaborate, neurotic necessity to hide the black man's true role in history.

And today the white man is faced head on with what is happening on the Black Continent, Africa. Look at the artifacts being discovered there, that are proving over and over again, how the black man had great, fine, sensitive civilizations before the white man was out of the caves. Below the Sahara, in the places where most of America's Negroes' foreparents were kidnapped, there is being unearthed some of the finest craftsmanship, sculpture and other objects, that has ever been seen by modern man. Some of these things now are on view in such places as New York City's Museum of Modern Art. Gold work of such fine tolerance and workmanship that it has no rival. Ancient objects produced by black hands . . . refined by those black hands with results that no human hand today can equal.

History has been so "whitened" by the white man that even the black professors have known little more than the most ignorant black man about the talents and rich civilizations and cultures of the black man of millenniums ago. I have lectured in Negro colleges and some of these brainwashed black Ph.D.'s, with their suspenders dragging the ground with degrees, have run to the white man's newspapers calling me a "black fanatic." Why, a lot of them are fifty years behind the times. If I were president of one of these black colleges, I'd hock the campus if I had to, to send a bunch of black students off digging in Africa for more, more and more proof of the black race's historical greatness. The white man now is in Africa digging and searching. An African elephant can't stumble without falling on some white man with a shovel. Practically every week, we read about some great new find from Africa's lost civilizations. All that's new is white science's attitude. The ancient civilizations of the black man have been buried on the Black Continent all the time.

Here is an example: A British anthropologist named Dr. Louis S. B. Leakey is displaying some fossil bones—a foot, part of a hand, some jaws, and skull fragments. On the basis of these, Dr. Leakey has said it's time to rewrite completely the history of man's origin.

This species of man lived 1,818,036 years before Christ. And these bones were found in Tanganyika. In the Black Continent.

It's a crime, the lie that has been told to generations of black men and white men both. Little innocent black children, born of parents who believed that their race had no history. Little black children seeing, before they could talk, that their parents considered themselves inferior. Innocent black children growing up, living out their lives, dying of old age—and all of their lives ashamed of being black. But the truth is pouring out of the bag now.

"In Conversation with Ernest J. Gaines"

Adrianne Bee

*This interview branches into the stories of Gaines's
early start as a reader and writer. Gaines, an African
American, was allowed to enter a library for the first
time in California, where he read dozens of books
about rural life and was drawn to work by John
Steinbeck and Willa Cather. Unable to find stories
about his culture in the segregated South, he realized
that he would have to begin writing them.*

In 1948, at the age of 15, Ernest Gaines left rural Oscar, Louisiana,
because there were no high schools for blacks near his home.
Carrying an old brown suitcase filled with some clothes, a bag of
oranges, teacakes and pralines, he left River Lake plantation, where
five generations of his family had lived in former slave quarters.

"If I had stayed in Louisiana much longer, I could have been hurt
and I could have given up on myself as so many of my colleagues
did," he says. "So many of my people here were defeated by the time
they were 18 or 19 years old. They just didn't have any hope to continue. They thought they would never amount to anything, never
do anything worthwhile with their lives. I could have been one of
those."

The son of sharecroppers, Gaines attended elementary school
in a one-room church where children knelt to write on pews and

worked in the fields during planting and harvesting seasons. They picked cotton, cut sugarcane and worked in dismal swamps. "I could never have written 'The Autobiography of Miss Jane Pittman' or 'A Gathering of Old Men' had I not lived it. But I wouldn't wish it on any other child," he says.

Following his parents' separation, Gaines was raised by his Aunt Augusteen, who gave him his first writing assignments. "Starting at 12 years old, she insisted I write letters for the old people on the plantation. They could neither read nor write because they never had the opportunity to go to school," he says. "So I wrote for them. Sometimes I had to create my own observations about their gardens, their cooking, the weather. I got a good feeling for character and voice."

Gaines carried memories of his people with him when he traveled to California to be with his mother and stepfather who had moved to Vallejo during World War II to find work. Escaping the segregated South, he was allowed to walk inside a public library for the first time. He read dozens of books about rural life and was drawn to John Steinbeck and Willa Cather—stories of people who worked the land. But he did not see *his* people and *his* land.

"I wanted to see on paper those Louisiana black children walking to school on cold days while Louisiana yellow buses passed them by. I wanted to see on paper those black parents going to work before the sun came up and coming back home to look after their children after the sun went down," Gaines remembers.

Working sometimes 15 hours a day, the teenage Gaines wrote by hand an interracial love story. Then on a rented typewriter, using two fingers, he completed the novel to his satisfaction. He cut the pages down to book size, tied them with string and mailed the package to a publishing house in New York.

"I thought it was a novel I had written. I thought they would put it between a couple covers and make it a book," he remembers. "They sent it back of course—still tied in the same string—so I burned it in the back yard."

Disappointed but determined, he kept writing. Sixteen years later a rewrite of this first manuscript would become his first published novel, "Catherine Carmier."

"My aunt taught me discipline and commitment. She was crippled and crawled on the floor her whole life, but she managed to do everything for us children," says Gaines, recalling the woman who ignored a welfare-donated wheelchair, gardened with a shortened hoe, and pulled her body across the yard to collect fallen pecans. Gaines dedicated "The Autobiography of Miss Jane Pittman," the story of a woman who has become a hero to thousands of readers, to his own hero. "My aunt was not able to walk a day in her life, but she taught me the importance of standing. I had to stand up and do things for my family as well as for my community. She taught me that standing is what it means to be somebody," he said.

Like his aunt, the characters in Gaines' short stories and novels have burdens, weight that would knock the average person down— and sometimes it does. Freedom, love, even life is lost.

What captures Gaines' imagination is how people manage to come through their struggles with dignity and grace. "When I speak to black students about Hemingway, they often ask me what I expect them to learn from 'that white man.' I tell them, 'All Hemingway wrote about was grace under pressure. And he was talking about you. Can you tell me a better example of grace under pressure than our people for the past 300 years?" Gaines asks.

"Grace under pressure doesn't necessarily mean facing a lion or a tiger. It's how anyone goes through their daily work, how they go through every day of their life, and go to a job they don't like to feed their children so they'll grow up to be a better generation."

You've said that at SFSU [San Francisco State University] you found good teachers who encouraged you to write.
The one person who influenced me the most was my composition teacher, Stanley Andersen. I was getting D's in Mr. Andersen's expository writing class, so I told him I wanted to write fiction. He

said, "This is not a fiction-writing class, but if you think you can improve yourself by writing fiction, then try it." I wrote "The Turtles" in his class, and he liked it very much. We keep in touch—but I still find it hard to call him Stan instead of Mr. Andersen.

Mr. Andersen passed on your story to other professors, and it was published in the first issue of *Transfer*, the University's literary magazine. Dorthea Oppenheimer, a literary agent from New York, was also impressed with your story.
She read "The Turtles" and asked to see my stories from that point on. Even though I didn't make her any money for many, many years, she sent out my stories while I was a student—and she kept all the rejection slips so I didn't have to see them. She died in 1987. She was my agent for 31 years.

What goals did you set for yourself after graduating from SFSU?
I gave myself 10 years to prove that I could write. It was the height of the Beat scene, but I didn't want to write about bohemian life. Most of what I wrote revolved around Louisiana. As Faulkner said, it's my "little postage stamp of native soil."

I had a few part-time jobs to support myself. I would write until two or three in the afternoon, then go to work at night. In seven years "Catherine Carmier" was published. "Of Love and Dust" followed three years later.

Did you find it difficult to stop writing and go to work?
When I was the night mail clerk at an insurance company, I used to sneak in the bathroom to write. I would write on paper towels and then when I got home, I would transfer [what I had written] to my notebook. After a while my boss found out what I was doing. He would knock on the door and I wouldn't come out. He'd start kicking on the door and he'd keep kicking. I'd say, "Don't you know you're disturbing a genius?"

And he'd say "Come out of there, genius." I'd do the work I had to do, but when I got a chance, I'd sneak back in there and write. I was writing "A Long Day in November." [Gaines managed to write 250 paper towels' worth of this story in the company men's room.]

How has Louisiana, your "little postage stamp of native soil," changed over the years?

When I left Louisiana in 1948, I could not have gone anywhere near the university where I teach today—not without going in the back door with a broom and a mop. And here I am a writer-in-residence since 1983. Doors that were once closed are open. At the same time, a few years back, the majority of whites in this state voted for a Klansman when David Duke was running for office. If it wasn't for the whites and all the blacks who voted against him, this man could have been senator or governor of this state. Many, many things have changed, but the elements of prejudice, racism—those things have a way of staying the same.

Any advice for young writers?

Six words and eight words: Read, read, read, write, write, write. And read, read, read, read, write, write, write, write. You must read in order to be a writer. Books are the main tool writers have to work with—not only the great classics, but contemporary novels as well. Writers need to keep up their antennae and open their minds. I always tell my students, "Look outside that window and look at all the green out there, all the trees and grass. There are so many different shades of that one color. That's how you should look at human beings." The most important thing, though, is to sit down at a desk and write for hours—and rewrite so someone can read your story a year, five years, or a hundred years later and still see exactly what you had intended them to see.

Do you believe that your writing is promoting understanding between blacks and whites?

Everybody is prejudiced in a way. There are good white characters, and there are evil ones. The same goes for the black characters: some are strong, some are weak. Every writer has a different perspective.

Last week I spoke with a white woman in North Carolina; she thought that Miss Jane Pittman was a better character than Dilsey in Faulkner's "The Sound and the Fury." She said that Miss Jane was deeper, more developed. I'm just giving my perspective. I got Miss Jane from Miss Jane's kitchen while Faulkner got Dilsey from his kitchen. She is free to tell you more in her own kitchen. I've put my opinion out there so that good teachers can help open students' minds to other perspectives.

Your characters often struggle with what it means to be a man. In "A Lesson Before Dying" Grant asks, "How am I supposed to tell him how to die when I don't even know how a man should live?" How would you answer his question?

Being a man is about responsibility. It's about giving to the world around you. It doesn't matter if a man's white, Hispanic, Asian or black. What matters is whether he treats other men with dignity and respect. Does he show bravery or does he turn his back like a coward? So many of my black characters have been denied their position as men, denied the opportunity to participate as full members of society. But they face that, stand on their two feet and fight. Everyone wants to be respected. All men like to stand in the sun one day in their life.

Can we look forward to another novel by Ernest Gaines?

Right now I'm not wrestling with the muse or the muse is not wrestling with me, but I'll get back to it. I do hope I'm never finished writing and still have something that I want to say at the very end. I don't think that a writer should ever feel finished or completely satisfied. You try to write another book, another story, you think maybe you can do it so much better the next time. You keep trying to get it perfect.

20

"Learning to Read"

Frances E. W. Harper

*Harper, an African American teacher, was born in
1825 in Baltimore, Maryland. In 1852, she took a
teaching position in Pennsylvania, where she lived in
an Underground Railroad station. Her experience
of the Underground Railroad and the movement of
slaves toward freedom had a deep effect on her
poetry. In 1854, she began giving antislavery
speeches throughout the northern United States
and Canada.*

Very soon the Yankee teachers
    Came down and set up school;
But, oh! how the Rebs did hate it,—
    It was agin' their rule.

Our masters always tried to hide
    Book learning from our eyes;
Knowledge didn't agree with slavery—
    'Twould make us all too wise.

But some of us would try to steal
    A little from the book,

And put the words together,
    And learn by hook or crook.

I remember Uncle Caldwell,
    Who took pot liquor fat
And greased the pages of his book,
    And hid it in his hat.

And had his master ever seen
    The leaves upon his head,
He'd have thought them greasy papers,
    But nothing to be read.

And there was Mr. Turner's Ben,
    Who heard the children spell,
And picked the words right up by heart,
    And learned to read 'em well.

Well, the Northern folks kept sending
    The Yankee teachers down;
And they stood right up and helped us,
    Though Rebs did sneer and frown.

And, I longed to read my Bible,
    For precious words it said;
But when I begun to learn it,
    Folks just shook their heads,

And said there is no use trying,
    Oh! Chloe, you're too late;
But as I was rising sixty,
    I had no time to wait.

So I got a pair of glasses,
    And straight to work I went,
And never stopped till I could read
    The hymns and Testament.

Then I got a little cabin
    A place to call my own—
And I felt as independent
    As the queen upon her throne.

21

"Precious Words"

Emily Dickinson

*This poem is about how words can sustain the human
spirit. Dickinson, an American poet, was born in
1830. Her poetry was short and usually consisted of
four-line stanzas. Although she wrote close to two
thousand poems, only seven were published during
her lifetime.*

He ate and drank the precious words.
His spirit grew robust;
He knew no more that he was poor,
Nor that his frame was dust.

He danced along the dingy days,
And this bequest of wings
Was but a book. What liberty
A loosened spirit brings!

"Learning to Read and Write," from *Frederick Douglass: Narrative of the Life of Frederick Douglass, an American Slave*

Frederick Douglass

Douglass relates the story of how he learned to read and write at a time when slaves were not allowed to go to school. He shows us how enterprising and clever he was in figuring out how he could get others to teach him just enough so that he could secretly continue learning on his own. Douglass knew that the way to freedom was through learning how to read and write.

I lived in Master Hugh's family about seven years. During this time, I succeeded in learning to read and write. In accomplishing this, I was compelled to resort to various stratagems. I had no regular teacher. My mistress, who had kindly commenced to instruct me, had, in compliance with the advice and direction of her husband, not only ceased to instruct, but had set her face against my being instructed by any one else. It is due, however, to my mistress to say of her, that she did not adopt this course of treatment immediately. She at first lacked the depravity indispensable to shutting me up in mental darkness. I was at least necessary for her to have some training in the exercise of irresponsible power, to make her equal to the task of treating me as though I were a brute.

My mistress was, as I have said, a kind and tender-hearted woman; and in the simplicity of her soul she commenced, when I first went to live with her, to treat me as she supposed one human being ought to treat another. In entering upon the duties of a slave-holder, she did not seem to perceive that I sustained to her the relation of a mere chattel, and that for her to treat me as a human being was not only wrong, but dangerously so. Slavery proved as injurious to her as it did to me. When I went there, she was a pious, warm, and tender-hearted woman. There was no sorrow or suffering for which she had not a tear. She had bread for the hungry, clothes for the naked, and comfort for every mourner that came within her reach. Slavery soon proved its ability to divest her of these heavenly qualities. Under its influence, the tender heart became stone, and the lamblike disposition gave way to one of tiger-like fierceness. The first step in her downward course was in her ceasing to instruct me. She now commenced to practice her husband's precepts. She finally became even more violent in her opposition than her husband himself. She was not satisfied with simply doing as well as he had commanded; she seemed anxious to do better. Nothing seemed to make her more angry than to see me with a newspaper. She seemed to think that here lay the danger. I have had her rush at me with a face made all up of fury, and snatch from me a newspaper, in a manner that fully revealed her apprehension. She was an apt woman; and a little experience soon demonstrated, to her satisfaction, that education and slavery were incompatible with each other.

From this time I was most narrowly watched. If I was in a separate room any considerable length of time, I was sure to be suspected of having a book, and was at once called to give an account of myself. All this, however, was too late. The first step had been taken. Mistress, in teaching me the alphabet, had given me the *inch*, and no precaution could prevent me from taking the *ell*.

The plan which I adopted, and the one by which I was most successful, was that of making friends of all the little white boys whom I met in the street. As many of these as I could, I converted into teachers. With their kindly aid, obtained at different times and in different places, I finally succeeded in learning to read. When I was sent on errands, I always took my book with me, and by doing one part of my errand quickly, I found time to get a lesson before my return. I used also to carry bread with me, enough of which was always in the house, and to which I was always welcome; for I was much better off in this regard than many of the poor white children in our neighborhood. This bread I used to bestow upon the hungry little urchins, who, in return, would give me that more valuable bread of knowledge. I am strongly tempted to give the names of two or three of those little boys, as a testimonial of the gratitude and affection I bear them; but prudence forbids;—not that it would injure me, but it might embarrass them; for it is almost an unpardonable offence to teach slaves to read in this Christian country. It is enough to say of the dear little fellows, that they lived on Philpot Street, very near Durgin and Bailey's ship-yard. I used to talk this matter of slavery over with them. I would sometimes say to them, I wished I could be as free as they would be when they got to be men. "You will be free as soon as you are twenty-one, *but I am a slave for life!* Have not I as good a right to be free as you have?" These words used to trouble them; they would express for me the liveliest sympathy, and console me with the hope that something would occur by which I might be free.

I was now about twelve years old, and the thought of being *a slave for life* began to bear heavily upon my heart. Just about this time, I got hold of a book entitled "The Columbian Orator." Every opportunity I got, I used to read this book. Among much of other interesting matter, I found in it a dialogue between a master and his slave. The slave was represented as having run away from his master three times. The dialogue represented the conversation which took place between them, when the slave was retaken the third time. In this dialogue, the whole argument in behalf of slavery was brought forward by the master, all of which was disposed of by the slave. The slave was made to say some very smart as well as impressive things in reply to his master—things which had the desired though unexpected effect; for the conversation resulted in the voluntary emancipation of the slave on the part of the master.

In the same book, I met with one of Sheridan's mighty speeches on and in behalf of Catholic emancipation. These were choice documents to me. I read them over and over again with unabated interest. They gave tongue to interesting thoughts of my own soul, which had frequently flashed through my mind, and died away for want of utterance. The moral which I gained from the dialogue was the power of truth over the conscience of even a slaveholder. What I got from Sheridan was a bold denunciation of slavery, and a powerful vindication of human rights. The reading of these documents enabled me to utter my thoughts, and to meet the arguments brought forward to sustain slavery; but while they relieved me of one difficulty, they brought on another even more painful than the one of which I was relieved. The more I read, the more I was led to abhor and detest my enslavers. I could regard them in no other light than a band of successful robbers, who had left their homes, and gone to Africa, and stolen us from our homes, and in a strange land reduced us to slavery. I loathed them as being the meanest as well as the most wicked of men. As I read and contemplated the subject, behold! that very discontentment which Master Hugh had predicted would follow my learning to read had already come, to torment and sting my soul to unutterable anguish. As I writhed under it, I would at times feel that learning to read had been a curse rather than a blessing. It had given me a view of my wretched condition, without the remedy. It opened my eyes to the horrible pit, but to no ladder upon which to get out. In moments of agony, I envied my fellow-slaves for their stupidity. I have often wished myself a beast. I preferred the condition of the meanest reptile to my own. Any thing, no matter what, to get rid of thinking! It was this everlasting thinking of my condition that tormented me. There was no getting rid of it. It was pressed upon me by every object within sight or hearing, animate or inanimate. The silver trump of freedom had roused my soul to eternal wakefulness. Freedom now appeared, to disappear no more forever. It was heard in every sound, and seen in everything. It was ever present to torment me with a sense of my wretched condition. I saw nothing without seeing it, I heard nothing without hearing it, and felt nothing without feeling it. It looked from every star, it smiled in every clam, breathed in every wind, and moved in every storm.

I often found myself regretting my own existence, and wishing myself dead; and but for the hope of being free, I have no doubt but that I should have killed myself, or done something for which I should have been killed. While in this state of mind, I was eager to hear any one speak of slavery. I was a ready listener. Every little while, I could hear something about the abolitionists. It was some time before I found what the word meant. It was always used in such connections as to make it an interesting word to me. If a slave ran away and succeeded in getting clear, or if a slave killed his master, set fire to a barn, or did any thing very wrong in the mind of a slaveholder, it was spoken of as the fruit of *abolition*. Hearing the word in this connection very often, I set about learning what it meant. The dictionary afforded me little or no help. I found it was "the act of abolishing"; but then I did not know what was to be abolished. Here I was perplexed. I did not dare to ask any one about its meaning, for I was satisfied that it was something they wanted me to know very little about. After a patient waiting, I got one of our city papers, containing an account of the number of petitions from the north, praying for the abolition of slavery in the District of Columbia, and of the slave trade between the States. From this time I understood the words *abolition* and *abolitionist*, and always drew near when that word was spoken, expecting to hear something of importance to myself and fellow-slaves. The light broke in upon me by degrees. I went one day down on the wharf of Mr. Waters; and seeing two Irishmen unloading a scow of stone, I went, unasked, and helped them. When we had finished, one of them came to me and asked me if I were a slave. I told him I was. He asked, "Are ye a slave for life?" I told him that I was. The good Irishman seemed to be deeply affected by the statement. He said to the other that it was a pity so fine a little fellow as myself should be a slave for life. He said it was a shame to hold me. They both advised me to run away to the north; that I should find friends there, and that I should be free. I pretended not to be interested in what they said, and treated them as if I did not understand them; for I feared they might be treacherous. White men have been known to encourage slaves to escape, and then, to get the reward, catch them and return them to their masters. I was afraid that these seemingly good men might use me so; but I nevertheless remembered their advice, and from that time I resolved to run away. I looked forward to time at which it would be safe for me to escape. I was too young to think of doing so immediately; besides, I wished to learn how to write, as I might have occasion to write my own pass. I consoled myself with the hope that I should one day find a good chance. Meanwhile, I would learn to write.

The idea as to how I might learn to write was suggested to me by being in Durgin and Bailey's ship-yard, and frequently seeing the ship carpenters, after hewing, and getting a piece of timber ready for use, write on the timber the name of that part of the ship for which it was intended. When a piece of timber was intended for the larboard side, it would be marked thus—"L." When a piece was for the starboard side, it would be marked thus—"S." A piece for the larboard side forward, would be marked thus—"L. F." When a piece was for starboard side forward, it would be marked thus—"S. F." For larboard aft, it would be marked thus—"L. A." For starboard aft, it would be marked thus—"S. A." I soon learned the names of these letters, and for what they were intended when placed upon a piece of timber in the ship-yard. I immediately commenced copying them, and in a short time was able to make the four letters named. After that, when I met with any boy who I knew could write, I would tell him I could write as well as he. The next word would be, "I don't believe you. Let me see you try it." I would then make the letters which I had been so fortunate as to learn, and ask him to beat that. In this way I got a good many lessons in writing, which it is quite possible I should never have gotten in any other way. During this time, my copy-book was the board fence, brick wall, and pavement;

my pen and ink was a lump of chalk. With these, I learned mainly how to write. I then commenced and continued copying the Italics in Webster's Spelling Book, until I could make them all without looking on the book. By this time, my little Master Thomas had gone to school, and learned how to write, and had written over a number of copy-books. These had been brought home, and shown to some of our near neighbors, and then laid aside. My mistress used to go to class meeting at the Wilk Street meetinghouse every Monday afternoon, and leave me to take care of the house. When left thus, I used to spend the time in writing in the spaces left in Master Thomas's copy-book, copying what he had written. I continued to do this until I could write a hand very similar to that of Master Thomas. Thus, after a long, tedious effort for years, I finally succeeded in learning how to write.

23

"India's Literacy Miracle"

This selection is about India's efforts, with the help of the United Nations Educational Scientific and Cultural Organization, to teach people who live in rural areas to read and write. The campaign, begun in 1990, sought to demonstrate that illiteracy in developing countries could be overcome by the year 2000. One of the most interesting results of the focus on teaching reading and writing is that as the level of education for women rises, both birth and child mortality rates fall.

Squatting on the ground in her faded sari, a piece of paper before her, Shakuntala clenches a pencil in her chapped and overworked hand. She begins to draw squiggles. It is Malayalam, the script of Kerala State in southern India, where she lives. "We need plumbing so that we will not get sick anymore," writes Shakuntala. It is the first petition of her life, and it is addressed to the district chief.

Shakuntala is in her mid-40s. She works as a day laborer on a plantation. She has never attended school. A year ago she could neither read nor write. Now she can, even though she makes many mistakes. For the first time in her life she worked her way through a newspaper. "I did not know how big the world was," she says. "Much bigger than on television."

Shakuntala took part in a program that demonstrated that miracles are possible. In just one year, the inhabitants of an entire district in India (more than 200,000 people—all between ages five and 65) learned to read and write. The town of Ernakulam in Kerala became the only place in the Third World with a literacy rate of 100 percent.

The initiators of the *Sakasharata Yagnam*, or literacy campaign, seek to demonstrate that illiteracy in the Third World can be overcome. Above all, the people of Ernakulam have shown that learning to read and write is not simply a matter of spending money, a frequent claim whenever new data on rising illiteracy come out, as they did at the United Nations Educational Scientific and Cultural Organization (UNESCO) conference in Thailand at which 1990 was proclaimed the year of world literacy.

UNESCO's ambitious goal of teaching 1 billion illiterates around the world to read and write by the year 2000 has been set in motion. In India alone, 64 percent of the population is unable to read or write. It is no consolation to this proud nation, with its great cultural heritage, that four countries in Asia have even worse statistics: Pakistan, Nepal, Bangladesh, and Afghanistan. But India lags far behind China, Indonesia, Sri Lanka, and even Burma.

Women are the greatest victims. In the Third World, 48.9 percent of them can neither read nor write. Among men, the figure is 27.9 percent. The illiteracy figures for India are 71.1 percent of the women and 42.8 percent of the men. "If more women went to school in our country, we would have 600 million people instead of 850 million," says Sam Pitroda, who heads the national literacy program. As the level of education of Third World women rises, the child mortality rate and the birthrate decline.

"Every developmental directive is closely tied to reading and writing," Pitroda says. "Why doesn't development fare well in the countryside? Because that is where the majority of the illiterates are. Why doesn't family planning work? Because the women cannot read or write."

"Each one teach one" is the new slogan of the literacy campaign. To the chagrin of some bureaucrats, Pitroda found that nationally sponsored programs did not catch on. "We have some 4 million students at our universities and about 1.6 million pupils in classes from the ninth to the twelfth grade. If each of them teaches just one person to read and write in the course of the year, it is a beginning."

That campaign is already in progress in many parts of the country, including New Delhi. Neeraj Bali, a ninth grader who is studying with a 28-year-old laundry worker, sometimes finds it difficult to give up free time, but he believes that "it is a national disgrace for people to have to sign with their thumb print."

The government in New Delhi thinks that it will take two years to reach a minimal level of literacy, despite the great willingness to learn and the industriousness of India's illiterate people. There is the fear that many might drop out. That is why people are saying, "Be quick and rigorous." This is perhaps more plausible in Kerala than elsewhere, because of Kerala's traditions.

The people of Kerala elected a communist government in 1957. They are proud of their progressive social politics, their agrarian reform, and their health system, which is the envy of the other Indian states. The life-expectancy in Kerala of 76 years is the highest in India, as is the literacy rate of 71 percent.

The miracle of writing began in Kottayam, a town of 70,000 in Kerala, located amid tea and coffee plantations. It boasts a dozen high schools, four colleges, and one full-fledged university. Its literacy rate was 86 percent two years ago, a national record. Still, there were 2,029 illiterates—but they were taught to read and write in just 100 days by 1,024 volunteers.

Volunteers repeated the example of Kottayam in Ernakulam in an enormous campaign that involved house visits, street theater, songs, marches, and educational lectures. In Kerala, people believe that there could soon be many more Shakuntalas if only the right starting point is found.

24

"Interrogation,"
from *Son of the Revolution*

Liang Heng, Judith Shapiro

*It is the time of China's Cultural Revolution when a
fifteen-year-old boy breaks into a locked storeroom of
books at his school and discovers the excitement of
reading. He forms a literary group with his friends
and writes poetry and letters. Suddenly, he is accused
of being a counterrevolutionary. He is locked in an
office and interrogated about everything he has read
and written. As he puzzles his way to the truth of
why he was singled out, he confronts a society intent
on suppressing the power of words.*

Soon after Liang Wei-ping left, Father returned to his work on
the Propaganda Team and I went back to school to begin the
new semester. My sister's stories had influenced me, and I resolved
to improve my relationship with the peasant children. This was
relatively easy to do, for I understood them very well. I knew they
were more afraid of ghosts than of anything else, and I used to im-
press them by nonchalantly visiting places they believed haunted.
My classmates were already a little afraid of me because of my height
and toughness; now they began to see me as some sort of hero.

What really kept me out of fights was the discovery of the
boarded-up storeroom. It was a flat-roofed building near the basketball court, and an idle moment's investigation through the cracks

in the door revealed that it was full of books, probably from the pre–Cultural Revolution school library. I hadn't read a good book since the Red Guards' search raid more than four years earlier, and my heart pounded. I quickly organized my handful of best friends, now including two peasant boys, and swore them to secrecy. Late that night, we pried off a few boards and climbed in. The acrid dust and mildew irritated our throats, and spiderwebs were everywhere; the books lay in broken piles, and the yellow paper bindings were sticky to the touch. But I felt as though we had entered paradise!

Someone had a flashlight, and we passed it about with shaking hands as we made our selections. We rationed ourselves, as we did when we stole sweet potatoes, for fear of being discovered. I chose a history of Europe and translations of Hegel's *Dialectics* and Flaubert's *Madame Bovary*. We replaced the boards carefully when we left.

It seemed there would be no end to our secret new pleasures. My life changed completely. I read with a passion I had felt for nothing else, keeping a diary about everything. The world of the imagination opened to me; I had new dreams and ambitions. My fellow thieves and I held discussions on literature and even began to write poetry, meeting on the windy riverbank but never feeling cold. We were a small literary society of fifteen-year-olds.

One day a classmate—I never found out who—took one of my poems from my desk and turned it in to a political cadre. It was a pessimistic poem, about my road of life leading nowhere. I was publicly criticized, and "dissatisfied with reality" was written in my file. Even that didn't quell my literary fervor. I simply began to turn it outward, writing letters to faraway friends and family like Little Li, who was still in Changsha because his parents had not yet been "liberated" from the study class. I developed quite an active correspondence, receiving answers to all my letters except those to Peng Ming. I imagined he must be too busy making Revolution to write.

Then one Saturday morning, classes were canceled for a special schoolwide meeting. New slogans were up in the big classroom, all of them dealing with class struggle, so we knew something important was in the air.

The political work group was the section of the school Revolutionary Committee with the real power, and Liu Guo-rong, a graduate of the Hunan Teachers' College's Politics Department, was the head of it. This was his meeting, and he strode to the podium as if girding himself for a performance.

It was a short meeting, but an exciting one. Liu's gold fillings sparkled in his expressive mouth, and a fine spray of saliva rained into the first rows at emphatic moments. A new movement was on, he told us, to round up the counterrevolutionary "May Sixteenth" conspirators.

"This nationwide secret organization has tried to attack our beloved Premier Zhou En-lai by sabotaging diplomatic relations with foreign countries," he bellowed. "They have a manifesto and a plan. Their activities are vicious. They use our postal system to spread their pernicious conspiracy everywhere." Liu paused, and we held our breaths. Finally he hissed, "We have a May Sixteenth conspirator right here in this room!"

Pandemonium broke as we chattered excitedly and craned our heads about hoping to identify the culprit. My mind raced down the list of my simple country teachers, but it seemed impossible that any of them should be involved in something so terrifying, so dangerous. Liu continued, "After the meeting, the counterrevolutionary will come to my office and surrender. I will put up five locked boxes throughout the school so that those of you who think they have spotted other counterrevolutionary activities can put in their reports. Don't worry, I am the only person with the keys. No one will know about your suspicions but you and me." He flashed his golden smile. "Meeting dismissed."

In the classroom, I held a whispered consultation with the members of my literary group and we decided to disband and return the stolen books that evening. Other classmates were checking their desks to make sure nothing had been planted there. Then I felt a hand on my shoulder. It was Teacher Deng, a member of the school Revolutionary Committee. "Liang Heng," he said, "Liu Guo-rong wants to see you."

I hurried behind him past my classmates' stares, shame burning me. A direct confrontation with Liu Guo-rong was too terrible to contemplate. I couldn't imagine what I had done.

The political work office held nothing but locked cabinets from floor to ceiling, the slogans on the walls, and some wooden chairs and a large desk. Liu sat behind this, smoking, a thick folder in front of him. He jerked his head toward an empty chair, and I sat down, trembling. Then he almost smiled.

"Did you forget to bring your ears with you this morning? You wanted a personal invitation?"

I flushed deeper in an agony of confusion.

"Well, you can still confess your activities as a May Sixteenth conspirator," said Liu, gesturing to a sheaf of blank papers on which I now noticed the heading "Confession" in big black characters.

My protests were useless. Liu shook his folder at me and claimed he knew everything, while I racked my brains for what the contents might be. Finally, he stood up and said, "You won't be leaving here until you've confessed, so you might as well begin now. Someone will bring you your lunch." I heard the key turn in the lock after him.

That morning the sounds of my classmates' voices rang in the corridors and I glued myself to the barred window hoping to catch a glimpse of a friend. I enumerated the possibilities over and over, rejecting them all: Could it be the books I had sent to Little Li in Changsha? Our literary group? The stolen sweet potatoes?

At noon, Teacher Deng came with food, and he whispered kindly to me, "You better confess, or heaven knows what will happen. The letter came from the Peking Public Security Bureau."

That explained it. Peng Ming must be in some kind of trouble. If I had come to the notice of Peking, things looked very bad for me indeed. But I recalled the content of my letters, and felt a bit calmer.

I had done nothing but speak of our old friendship and ask Peng Ming if he could send me some materials on the arts; he was, after all, a composer.

Liu came back that afternoon to question me. His face was constantly changing, sometimes fierce, sometimes kind and smiling, until I felt numb and I wasn't really sure what was right anymore. On the one hand, he threatened me with jail; on the other, he promised me I could join the Communist Youth League if I only admitted my crime. "Your father came to the countryside with a black mark on his record, and before it's wiped clean you give him a counterrevolutionary son!" Liu said. "Think of the glory for your family if you tell the Party everything! Think how proud your father will be!"

At one point I mentioned Peng Ming's name. Liu lit up ecstatically. "Aha, you've confided the name of your counterrevolutionary contact to the Party! That's wonderful!" And he seized a piece of paper and, consulting his watch, noted down the exact moment of my "confession." Then he looked at me expectantly. "Go on."

I don't know how many times I explained the nature of my friendship with Peng Ming. I told Liu that we had been neighbors, that he had taken me with him on a New Long March. I explained that I had helped out in Peking, that his sister and my sister were classmates. But I insisted I knew nothing about any May Sixteenth conspiracy, nor that Peng Ming might have anything to do with counterrevolutionary activities. I didn't understand much of what was happening to me, but I thought I might as well die rather than confess something false that might be used against my friend.

In the late afternoon, Liu opened his folder and took out the letters I had written to Peking. I broke out in sweat then: I had never dreamed the Public Security Bureau could be so thorough.

"These letters were written in your own hand, right?" asked Liu.

"Of course," I responded. I described again the nature of my friendship with Peng Ming and my reasons for writing the letters.

Liu wasn't happy. "You're only a fifteen-year-old boy, and you dare take me for a three-year-old child," he said, rising and approaching me threateningly. He seized me at the base of the neck and squeezed. "Confess your counterrevolutionary plot!" he commanded.

It hurt so much I couldn't control my tears. "I've never heard of any May Sixteenth conspiracy." I sobbed. "I've told you everything I know."

And so it went, on and on in circles. They made me sleep there on the desk that night, and the next, and the next. Liu came to question me every afternoon, sometimes hitting me, sometimes flattering me and trying to bribe me with political favors. Teacher Deng brought me my meals, and was kind to me with cigarettes and information. I think what hurt me most during that time was the way my friends betrayed me.

Every time Liu came in, he had new "evidence" in his hand, reports pushed into the locked boxes by the people I had trusted most. The people I had defended in fights turned me in, the people with whom I had stolen food. My literary friends told of our book thefts and our poetry meetings; my homeroom teacher wrote about my "bad thought." And when I called out the window to my round-headed friend Little Wu, he looked frightened and hurried away. Every day I traced out the history of my relationship with Peng on the papers marked "Confession"; every day Liu took them away, muttering, "Another crime."

It was Teacher Deng who gave me the strength not to "confess" a lie. He explained that the letter from the Peking Security Bureau had asked only that I be investigated, not that I be arrested. Still, I knew that Liu would have me arrested if he could. It would be great Revolutionary glory if he could ferret out a big counterrevolutionary in his little country school, a great boost for his career. So every night I cried, torn between the desire not to hurt Peng Ming and the desire to protect Father from yet another disgrace.

On the fifth day, Liu didn't come until late in the day, and he had a plainclothes Public Security officer with him. "This is your last chance," he announced with satisfaction. "If you don't confess today, tomorrow you'll go to jail." Before my eyes, he went to a cabinet, unlocked it, and handed my file over to the officer.

That night, as I lay on my desk, I had no tears left. I had lived fifteen years, but I had no desire to live even one more. I had been the victim of political movements since the age of three, first through my mother, then through my father, and now through an absurd coincidence in my own affairs. Society hated me. It had turned me into an outcast and a thief. My stepmother disliked me and my father was a broken man. I even hated him for what he had done to our family.

I imagined the next day I would be brought to jail as a criminal, paraded through the streets as the peasants shouted, "Down with the counterrevolutionary!" My friends would be among them, throwing rocks and sticks, laughing at my shame, glad that now the country would be that much more secure than it had been before the criminal's arrest. Perhaps first there would be a public criticism meeting, a beating, a humiliation. . . .

The dusty dark lightbulb hanging several yards above me was still visible in the night. Suddenly, I realized that I could die. I could unscrew that lightbulb and put my hand there where the current flowed and I would be dead. I should never again be tormented by memories of Mother's humiliated and accepting face as Father cursed her for betraying the Party's faith in her; of Nai Nai's swollen cheeks as she lay in her black coffin; of Father kneeling before his burning books, praising the Party; of Liang Fang's feces-covered shoes as she came home to write her Thought Reports. I should never again hear the words "stinking intellectual's son," or lie on my stomach in the sweet potato fields; my throat wouldn't hurt anymore where Liu had squeezed it. I was amazed at the simplicity of it all.

The thought came quickly and I acted quickly. Standing on the table, I reached the bulb easily and it unscrewed smoothly into my hand. It was a lonely action, and I felt suddenly angry that it should

be so. There should have been someone to help me do it, or someone to urge me not to. I reflected bitterly that after my death the
mob would stone my body just as it would if I were alive, the difference being that now they would say that the counterrevolutionary had killed himself because of his crime. I would never be able
to explain to Father that I wasn't guilty, and I remembered his old,
sad face, weeping, telling himself to be patient and tolerant, that
someday his question would be made clear. Another thought struck
me with equal force: If I died, Peng Ming's enemies could invent my
confession, and use it against him just as if I had penned it with my
own hand.

The desire to live came strong then, stronger than the desire to
die. I remember Father excitedly recording the peasant boy's folk
song by torchlight, still a man of letters even in the midst of greatest trouble. I thought of Mother and Waipo, waiting for me in
Changsha, and Liang Wei-ping sharing her rice *baba* among the
peasants. The hoodlums had cared for me so well on the streets, and
Teacher Luo had forgiven me so graciously for the caricatures I had
drawn of him. There was so much good in this crazy world, but so
much more that was impossible to understand.

Why should two good people like my parents be forced to divorce each other? Why should Liang Fang raise a machine gun
against her fellow teenagers? Why did the peasants fear the cadres
so terribly if they were representatives of our great Communist
Party? Why were people so determined to make me and Peng Ming
look like counterrevolutionaries when we wanted only to make a
contribution to our country? Why had the Revolution given us all
so little when we had sacrificed everything for it?

That night, I resolved that I would seek the answers to these
questions. If I was to live, it would no longer be numbly and aimlessly. I would live bravely. I would not be like Father, denying the
facts and fooling himself, nor like Pockmark Liu, disillusioned and
cynical. I would go to prison, but I would study so that I could
understand why my country had produced such tragedies.

The next morning, Liu arrived, but he was alone. "You can go," he said dourly.

It was no wonder I believed in fate, my life was just that crazy. I thought I must be dreaming again, but I didn't want to question my luck. I stumbled out, blinking in the bright light.

Later, I learned that the Central Committee in Peking had issued a document saying that too many people were being arrested on May Sixteenth conspiracy charges, and that in fact the conspiracy was not so big. Liu had to let me go. Still, the incident was by no means easily forgotten. My classmates shunned me, and Liu had his ways of having his revenge. In my file he wrote, "Corresponded with person with serious political questions," and when my class finished lower middle school that spring, I was the only one not allowed to proceed to upper middle school. The reason: "Complicated Thought."

25

"Reign of the Reader"

M. Freeman

In Cuba during the mid-1800s, readers were hired to read out loud to highly skilled workers as they worked in cigar-making factories. For four hours each day, they read great literature, reports by radical social thinkers, and socially relevant stories. The workers controlled this practice, much to the consternation of the factory owners.

No one is certain of the exact place it started. But somewhere in 19th-century Cuba, people started reading to help bored manual laborers pass the time. The idea caught on, and in the island's fabled tobacco industry, the role of *el lector*, the reader, took hold.

Fashioning fine cigars by hand was demanding, meticulous work, certainly, but once learned it could not have been mentally stimulating. Conversation helped, but the reading—*la lectura*—helped more.

Gary Mormino, professor of history at University of South Florida, Tampa, has studied and written extensively about *la lectura*, and he stresses that it represented far more than entertainment during a repetitive job. The readers broadened the intellectual scope and sharpened the political outlook of the workers they read to. And those workers appreciated, even revered them for it.

The readers even helped shape history at the turn of the 20th century, when the institution was at its height. But even from its earliest beginnings, the practice was a threat to the status quo, and the factory owners knew it. But it took them half a century to stop it, because it was a practice that the workers themselves controlled from the beginning.

Self-Selected

From the beginning—readers were already well established in Cuban cigar factories by the 1860s—the workers decided what the readers would read and how much they would be paid. The workers paid the readers themselves, because from the beginning the factory owners were opposed to the idea, mostly because of the type of literature the workers wanted to hear.

The cigar makers were highly skilled and had a sense of solidarity, and could not be simply fired and replaced. The labor movement was a strong force in the late 19th century, and the cigar workers wanted to learn, as they worked, about the foremost thinkers in progressive politics. This did not sit well with the factory owners, but there was little they could do about it.

At the same time, revolutionaries were agitating to throw the Spanish colonial overlords out of Cuba. This unrest eventually pushed many cigar makers out of the island, and cigar factories sprang up in Key West, Florida, and particularly in a section of the city of Tampa that came to be known as Ybor City, for the cigar manufacturer Vicente Martínez Ybor.

Prose and Politics

There were cigar factories and readers in other places, but the heyday of the reader was certainly in Ybor City from the late 1880s to about 1930. There were hundreds of them active at any one time.

The practice had a certain formal structure. In some factories, the reader sat in a plain chair, but at many they had a platform on which the reader sat or stood. They typically read for about four hours a day.

The first hour was devoted to reading newspapers, which would be translated into Spanish by the readers if necessary. During the second hour, the reader read a serialized novel. This was "always the most significant act of the day," Mormino says.

The readers would assume the voices of the characters, acting out the dialogue and injecting as much drama and emotion as possible into their reading. The better able they were to do this, the more respect they were accorded.

Cervantes' *Don Quixote* was a perennial favorite, but also popular were such novelists of the day as Victor Hugo and Emile Zola. The work of these French social realists represented, at the time, a progressive political outlook.

The edge sharpened in the third hour, with what the readers called "political economy"—radical social thinkers such as Bakunin and Marx. The fourth hour was devoted to something like Shakespeare or a short story with a whimsical theme, always something light to end the day with, often a story by Benito Pérez-Galdós, whom Mormino described as "the O. Henry of Spain."

End of an Era

The readers were the superstars of their day and place, Mormino says, not least because they helped the cigar workers attain a degree of intellectual sophistication few manual laborers could hope to equal. The opportunity was not limited to men—women were present in the factories as well as men, and at least two women were active as readers.

The institution furthered the Cuban revolution against Spanish rule, since the readers and workers were strong supporters of the revolutionary movement and gave its leader, the brilliant writer José Martí, a hero's welcome when he visited Ybor City in 1891.

But by 1931, unsuccessful strikes had weakened the power of the cigar workers, the Depression had hurt cigar sales, and the owners settled on the readers as scapegoats and banned them. The workers went on strike to save their beloved readers, but the strike was broken and the readers' podiums torn down. The radio replaced the reader, and increasingly machines replaced the workers.

But the institution of *la lectura* still stands, Mormino says, not just as an historical curiosity but as an "almost unique" example of how merely reading aloud could be so strongly loved, so fiercely defended, and how such a deep love of the life of the mind could be instilled in people who labored with their hands and empowered their intellects in those hot Florida factories in the days, gone forever, of *el lector*—the reader.

Part III

How We Read

Selections describe the different ways our minds work as we try to understand what we read.

26

"Gerald Eisman,"
from *Speaking of Reading*

Gerald Eisman

*A mathematician-turned-computer-science-professor,
Eisman surrenders to what he describes as his abstract
mode when reading technical material. Here he
compares reading, which is abstract because it deals
with symbolic representations of words, to his
profession, which is abstract because it deals with
symbolic representations of mechanical processes.*

Did you read *Calvin and Hobbes* today? When we were kids, Sunday was an event in my home. We would rush to get the newspaper, spread it out on the floor, and fight over who would get to the funnies first. Now I fight over them with my own kids. Doesn't everyone fight over the funnies? I won't buy a newspaper unless it has *Doonesbury*.

Other than the funnies, I read economics, philosophy, and books in my profession. I especially enjoy playing mental games while reading in the technical, abstract fields. I don't read much fiction. I notice how much time my wife takes to read a novel; that's the time I'll take to play with my children or watch ball on television.

I like to read about the theoretical foundations of computer science, both historical and current. I'm also interested in hardware developments. I'm interested in the way the theory of computer science is being developed using a mathematical approach, using mathematical language, using the way mathematicians think.

Right now I'm reading a book on computers called *Parallel Program Design*. I haven't always liked computers, but I've been around them since their beginnings. I actually used to find them too pedestrian, too down to earth, machinelike. That reaction wasn't uncommon among mathematicians in the '60s and '70s. Now there's a tremendous amount of action in the computer science field. A whole evolution has occurred over the last twelve years that has encouraged a lot of people like myself to switch from math to computers.

After years of reading technical, abstract material, I can put myself into an abstract mode fairly easily. Much of mathematics involves a series of definitions and theorems. The idea is to make the definitions so precise and so clear that the theorems flow naturally from the definitions. The problem is that if the distinctions become too precise, if they lose their generality, they become meaningless.

When I read something new, I have to adjust my perspective on the material so I know how large a step the author expects me to take. Reading, like any activity, is preceded by certain expectations. Most of the time, one is not even aware of the expectations until there's some sort of breakdown in them. For example, I was reading something yesterday in which the authors were designing a logical system to prove the correctness of programs they were writing. Some common steps in their proofs were occurring over and over again. If a phenomenon is common enough to repeat itself frequently, it is often given a name and then it is referred to by that name. These authors named one of the logical constructs "unless": something was true unless something else was true. As I was reading through the examples, each one had a certain abstract idea of "unlessness." Each proof took a few minutes to read carefully and to understand fully. Then I came upon one that was very simple; it only took a second to figure out. I had already prepared myself for thirty seconds of concentrated thought for each new concept, so I stopped and wondered, "Why did they bother with that? It was so simple." It threw me off completely.

In the course of reading, I develop expectations about what's going to come next. Sometimes, when I read a book by two authors, I can tell when the second author has written a chapter. Suddenly, after having read one author's writing, my expectation of what will be developed next doesn't match the text. I'm thrown off, my strategies are wrong. I'm not even aware I had any expectations up to that point.

I often read a chapter of a computer science book thinking, "Can I make a lecture out of this? Would this take up an hour and fifteen minutes?" I read that way often. I read what interests me, and I also teach what interests me. I'll read about a hundred pages of a book to get the big picture, then go back and read it a second time for details, for examples. My teaching is done by jumping back and forth from theorem to example. I try to be practical for my students, as solid as I can be, rather than too abstract. When I read a textbook for myself only, I usually don't read the examples very carefully. I understand the abstraction, so I'll skim through the examples pretty quickly.

I get very involved reading technical material. It's tiring to read— it's not the type of material I can't put down. An hour session gives me a lot to digest, and it can really inspire me. After that hour, I play with the thoughts I've gained and synthesize them into other ideas I may be working on. I think about how they apply to a curriculum I'm developing, or to the research I'm carrying out in computer science. I'll take the author's abstractions, approach, and manner of thinking, and abstract from them. I mull them over in my mind.

Usually I have two or three technical books going at one time. The books tend to be in different areas within computer science. It's less tiring to read several different authors at a time because they all have different approaches. I like the diversification; it's like stretching between courses. I choose books by browsing through top-rate bookstores which carry current books. I love to look at all the titles—there are always a few that seem exciting. I have one close friend in the field with whom I share titles. We'll exchange books and talk about them together.

Reading is fundamental to what I do. Without reading about new ideas, and attacking new concepts and being replenished by them, my job would be incredibly dull.

"The Voice You Hear When You Read Silently," from *New and Selected Poems*

Thomas Lux

This poem captures a definition of reading as it compares reading to the voice in one's own head. The voice, however, is more than just the sound of the words.

The voice you hear when you read silently
is not silent, it is a speaking-
out-loud voice in your head: it is *spoken*,
a voice is *saying* it
as you read. It's the writer's words,
of course, in a literary sense
his or her "voice" but the sound
of that voice is the sound of *your* voice.
Not the sound your friends know
or the sound of a tape played back
but your voice
caught in the dark cathedral
of your skull, your voice heard
by an internal ear informed by internal abstracts
and what you know by feeling,
having felt. It is your voice
saying, for example, the word "barn"
that the writer wrote

but the "barn" you say
is a barn you know or knew. The voice
in your head, speaking as you read,
never says anything neutrally—some people
hated the barn they knew,
some people love the barn they know
so you hear the word loaded
and a sensory constellation
is lit: horse-gnawed stalls,
hayloft, black heat tape wrapping
a water pipe, a slippery
spilled *chirrr* of oats from a split sack,
the bony, filthy haunches of cows . . .
And "barn" is only a noun—no verb
or subject has entered into the sentence yet!
The voice you hear when you read to yourself
is the clearest voice: you speak it
speaking to you.

28

"The Birth of an Alchemist," from *Better Than Life*

Daniel Pennac

Pennac writes about learning to write and read the word mommy *from the point of view of a small child. Step by step, we are led to the glorious moment for the child when the separate worlds of form and meaning become one, and the written word breaks forth.*

School came just in time.
It took responsibility for the future.

Reading, writing, arithmetic.

At the beginning, he went at it with real enthusiasm.

How amazing that those tails and circles and little bridges joined together formed real letters! And that those letters could make syllables, and those syllables, one after the other, words. He couldn't believe it. And that some of those words were familiar to him—it was magical!

Mommy, for example, *mommy*, three little bridges, a circle, then three more little bridges done twice, then two slanting sticks, and the result was *mommy*. How could such a wonder ever cease to amaze him?

Try to picture the moment. He got up early. He was with his mother, the one whose name he would soon be writing, he went out into the autumn drizzle (yes, an autumn drizzle, the light was the color of an uncleaned aquarium, let's not skip on the dramatic details), he headed for the school still wrapped in the warmth of his bed, the taste of cereal in his mouth, tightly holding the hand just above his head, walking as quickly as he could, taking two steps for his mother's one, his little knapsack bouncing on his back, then came the school door, the rapid kiss goodbye, the asphalt playground with its row of maples, the clanging bell . . . at first he took shelter from the rain under the overhang, then he joined the schoolyard games, but a few minutes later they all found themselves sitting behind Lilliputian desks, quiet and no moving around, all the body's movements concentrated on the effort of moving the pencil down this low-ceilinged corridor called the line. Tongue stuck out, fingers numb and wrist stiff . . . little bridges, circles, tails, sticks, more little bridges . . . he is miles from his mother now, lost in this strange solitude called *effort,* in the company of all those other solitudes with their tongues stuck out . . . and now the first letters are assembled . . . lines of "a's," lines of "m's," of "q's" (the "q" is no joke with its diving, backwards tail, but it's a piece of cake compared to the "s" with its treacherous curves, and the "k" with its spray of lines shooting out every which way), all the difficult ones conquered so that, little by little, as if they were magnetized, the letters come together spontaneously into syllables, lines of *mom* and *dad,* and the syllables in turn making words . . .

Then, one day, his ears still humming from the commotion of the lunchroom, he contemplated the silent flowering of the word on white paper, there, before his eyes: *mommy.*

He'd seen it on the blackboard, of course, and recognized it, but now, right here, he had written it with his own hand.

In a voice that quavered at first, he stumbled over the two syllables, separately. "Mom-my."

Then, suddenly, he understood.

"Mommy!"

His triumphant cry celebrated the culmination of the greatest intellectual voyage ever, a sort of first step on the moon, the movement from an arbitrary set of lines to the most emotionally charged meaning. Little bridges, circles and slanting sticks . . . and you could say "Mommy!" There it was, written, right there, and he had done it! Not a combination of syllables, not a word or a concept anymore. It wasn't *any* mother, it was *his* mother, a magical transformation, infinitely more eloquent than the most faithful photographic likeness, built from nothing but little circles and sticks and bridges, that have now suddenly—and forever!—become more than scratches on paper. They have become her presence, her voice, the good way she smelled this morning, her lap, that infinity of details, that wholeness, so intimately absolute, and so absolutely foreign to what is written there, on the rails of the page, within the four walls of the classroom.

Lead into gold.

Nothing less.

He had just turned lead into gold.

29

"Watch TV—In Your Head!"

Jennifer Liu

An eighth grader is asked to write an essay about reading. Liu, a competent and experienced young reader, lays out a simple and succinct plan to help others read better.

Have you ever been stuck where you are bored because you can't watch television? Well, here's your answer—read. It's like watching television in your head, except you have to use your brain to get the story. There are so many genres of books, why not read a book? Just pick your choice.

To get started, find a book that seems really interesting and appealing to you; don't get something that you will quit reading within a few short minutes. Try a nice and long book about a topic you really like—perhaps a romance, horror, or fantasy. Then find a comfortable place to sit where you won't be disturbed; a quiet spot is the best place to let your mind read and sink into a book.

Now that you have gotten all of your equipment and settled down, let's put some additional issues into consideration. If you think that you may not be comfortable while you are reading because you are cold or too warm, take care of those problems beforehand. You may want to grab a drink or snack; therefore, you won't have to in between reading. Also, make sure you have enough light so you don't hurt your eyes.

Too used to watching television? Not to worry because all you need to read your wonderful book is an undivided attention and a 100% focus on reading your book. While you are reading the story, try to imagine the scenes as you read. This helps you create a movie—in your head! You have the story in your hands, however, when you imagine the characters you can make them anyone or anything you want.

So, you have your guide on how to make reading a fun alternative to television. You should know that reading doesn't have to be a bad experience. It can be fun as long as you don't give up before you are a chapter into the book. Reading may also increase your thinking and writing skills because of exposure to correct grammar and punctuation usage.

30

"Tuning," from *The Winter Room*

Gary Paulsen

In this introduction to his novel The Winter Room, *Paulsen tantalizes readers with the sights, sounds, and smells of the story that is about to unfold. And then he reminds them that books need readers to come alive.*

If books could be more, could show more, could own more, this book would have smells. . . .

It would have the smells of old farms; the sweet smell of new-mown hay as it falls off the oiled sickle blade when the horses pull the mower through the field, and the sour smell of manure steaming in a winter barn. It would have the sticky-slick smell of birth when the calves come and they suck for the first time on the rich, new milk; the dusty smell of winter hay dried and stored in the loft waiting to be dropped down to the cattle; the pungent fermented smell of the chopped corn silage when it is brought into the manger on the silage fork. This book would have the smell of new potatoes sliced and frying in light pepper on a woodstove burning dry pine, the damp smell of leather mittens steaming on the back of the stovetop, and the acrid smell of the slop bucket by the door when the lid is lifted and the potato peelings are dumped in—but it can't.

Books can't have smells.

If books could be more and own more and give more, this book would have sound. . . .

It would have the high, keening sound of the six-foot bucksaws as the men pull them back and forth through the trees to cut pine for paper pulp; the grunting-gassy sounds of the work teams snorting and slapping as they hit the harness to jerk the stumps out of the ground. It would have the chewing sounds of cows in the barn working at their cuds on a long winter's night; the solid thunking sound of the ax coming down to split stovewood, and the piercing scream of the pigs when the knife cuts their throats and they know death is at hand—but it can't.

Books can't have sound.

And finally if books could be more, give more, show more, this book would have light. . . .

Oh, it would have the soft gold light—gold with bits of hay dust floating in it—that slips through the crack in the barn wall: the light of the Coleman lantern hissing flat-white in the kitchen; the silver-gray light of a middle winter day, the splattered, white-night light of a full moon on snow, the new light of dawn at the eastern edge of the pasture behind the cows coming in to be milked on a summer morning—but it can't.

Books can't have light.

If books could have more, give more, be more, show more, they would still need readers, who bring to them sound and smell and light and all the rest that can't be in books.

The book needs you.

31

"Superman and Me," from
The Most Wonderful Books: Writers on Discovering the Pleasures of Reading

Sherman Alexie

*Alexie grew up on an Indian reservation in eastern
Washington State. In this selection, he shares how he
came to reading at the age of three with the* Superman
*comics. He could not yet read the words so he supplied
those of his own.*

I learned to read with a *Superman* comic book. Simple enough, I suppose. I cannot recall which particular *Superman* comic book I read, nor can I remember which villain he fought in that issue. I cannot remember the plot, nor the means by which I obtained the comic book. What I can remember is this: I was three years old, a Spokane Indian boy living with his family on the Spokane Indian Reservation in eastern Washington state. We were poor by most standards, but one of my parents usually managed to find some minimum-wage job or another, which made us middle class by reservation standards. I had a brother and three sisters. We lived on a combination of irregular paychecks, hope, fear, and government-surplus food.

My father, who is one of the few Indians who went to Catholic school on purpose, was an avid reader of westerns, spy thrillers, murder mysteries, gangster epics, basketball-player biographies, and anything else he could find. He bought his books by the pound at Dutch's Pawn Shop, Goodwill, Salvation Army, and Value Village. When he had extra money, he bought new novels at supermarkets, convenience stores, and hospital gift shops. Our house was filled with books. They were stacked in crazy piles in the bathroom, bedrooms, and living room. In a fit of unemployment-inspired creative energy, my father built a set of bookshelves and soon filled them with a random assortment of books about the Kennedy assassination, Watergate, the Vietnam War, and the entire twenty-three book series of the Apache westerns. My father loved books, and since I loved my father with an aching devotion, I decided to love books as well.

I can remember picking up my father's books before I could read. The words themselves were mostly foreign, but I still remember the exact moment when I first understood, with a sudden clarity, the purpose of a paragraph. I didn't have the vocabulary to say "paragraph," but I realized that a paragraph was a fence that held words. The words inside a paragraph worked together for a common purpose. They had some specific reason for being inside the same fence. This knowledge delighted me. I began to think of everything in terms of paragraphs. Our reservation was a small paragraph within the United States. My family's house was a paragraph, distinct from the other paragraphs of the LeBrets to the north, the Fords to our south, and the Tribal School to the west. Inside our house, each family member existed as a separate paragraph, but still had genetics and common experiences to link us. Now, using this logic, I can see my changed family as an essay of seven paragraphs: mother, father, older brother, the deceased sister, my younger twin sisters, and our adopted little brother.

At the same time I was seeing the world in paragraphs, I also picked up that *Superman* comic book. Each panel, complete with picture, dialogue, and narrative, was a three-dimensional paragraph. In one panel, Superman breaks through a door. His suit is red, blue, and yellow. The brown door shatters into many pieces. I look at the narrative above the picture. I cannot read the words, but I assume it tells me that Superman is breaking down the door. Aloud, I pretend to read the words and say "Superman is breaking down the door." Words, dialogue, also float out of Superman's mouth. Because he is breaking down the door, I assume he says, "I am breaking down the door." Once again, I pretend to read the words and say aloud, "I am breaking down the door." In this way, I learned to read.

This might be an interesting story all by itself. A little Indian boy teaches himself to read at an early age and advances quickly. He reads *Grapes of Wrath* in kindergarten when other children are struggling through Dick and Jane. If he'd been anything but an Indian boy living on the reservation, he might have been called a prodigy. But he is an Indian boy living on the reservation, and is simply an oddity. He grows into a man who often speaks of his childhood in the third-person, as if it will somehow dull the pain and make him sound more modest about his talents.

A smart Indian is a dangerous person, widely feared and ridiculed by Indians and non-Indians alike. I fought with my classmates on a daily basis. They wanted me to stay quiet when the non-Indian teacher asked for answers, for volunteers, for help. We were Indian children who were expected to be stupid. Most lived up to those expectations inside the classroom, but subverted them on the outside. They struggled with basic reading in school, but could remember how to sing a few dozen powwow songs. They were monosyllabic in front of their non-Indian teachers, but could tell complicated stories and jokes at the dinner table. They submissively ducked their heads when confronted by a non-Indian adult, but would slug it out with the Indian bully who was ten years older. As Indian children, we were expected to fail in the non-Indian world. Those who failed were ceremonially accepted by other Indians and appropriately pitied by non-Indians.

I refused to fail. I was smart. I was arrogant. I was lucky. I read books late into the night, until I could barely keep my eyes open. I read books at recess, then during lunch, and in the few minutes left after I had finished my classroom assignments. I read books in the car when my family traveled to powwows or basketball games. In shopping malls, I ran to the bookstores and read bits and pieces of as many books as I could. I read the books my father brought home from the pawnshops and secondhand stores. I read the books I borrowed from the library. I read the backs of cereal boxes. I read the newspaper. I read the bulletins posted on the walls of the school, the clinic, the tribal offices, the post office. I read junk mail. I read auto-repair manuals. I read magazines. I read anything that had words and paragraphs. I read with equal parts joy and desperation. I loved those books, but I also knew that love had only one purpose. I was trying to save my life.

Despite all the books I read, I am still surprised I became a writer. I was going to be a pediatrician. These days, I write novels, short stories, and poems. I visit schools and teach creative writing to Indian kids. In all my years in the reservation school system, I was never taught how to write poetry, short stories, or novels. I was certainly never taught that Indians wrote poetry, short stories, and novels. Writing was something beyond Indians. I cannot recall a single time that a guest teacher visited the reservation. There must have been visiting teachers. Who were they? Where are they now? Do they exist? I visit the schools as often as possible. The Indian kids crowd the classroom. Many are writing their own poems, short stories, and novels. They have read my books. They have read many other books. They look at me with bright eyes and arrogant wonder. They are trying to save their lives. Then there are the sullen and already defeated Indian kids who sit in the back rows and ignore me with theatrical precision. The pages of their notebooks are empty. They carry neither pencil nor pen. They stare out the window. They refuse and resist. "Books," I say to them. "Books," I say. I throw my weight against their locked doors. The door holds. I am smart. I am arrogant. I am lucky. I am trying to save our lives.

32

"How to Mark a Book," from *The Mercury Reader*

Mortimer Adler

*Books need readers to have conversations with them,
to engage with them. In order for these conversations
to take place, readers need to write in books. "I
contend, quite bluntly," writes Adler, "that marking
up a book is not an act of mutilation but of love."
Adler presents ways for marking books in order to
help us become better readers, writers, and thinkers.*

You know you have to read "between the lines" to get the most out of anything. I want to persuade you to do something equally important in the course of your reading. I want to persuade you to "write between the lines." Unless you do, you are not likely to do the most efficient kind of reading.

I contend, quite bluntly, that marking up a book is not an act of mutilation but of love.

You shouldn't mark up a book which isn't yours. Librarians (or your friends) who lend you books expect you to keep them clean, and you should. If you decide that I am right about the usefulness of marking books, you will have to buy them. Most of the world's great books are available today, in reprint editions, at less than a dollar.

There are two ways in which you can own a book. The first is the property right you establish by paying for it, just as you pay for clothes and furniture. But this act of purchase is only the prelude to possession. Full ownership comes only when you have made it a part of yourself, and the best way to make yourself a part of it is by writing in it. An illustration may make the point clear. You buy a beefsteak and transfer it from the butcher's icebox to your own. But you do not own the beefsteak in the most important sense until you consume it and get it into your bloodstream. I am arguing that books, too, must be absorbed in your bloodstream to do you any good.

Confusion about what it means to *own* a book leads people to a false reverence for paper, binding, and type—a respect for the physical thing—the craft of the printer rather than the genius of the author. They forget that it is possible for a man to acquire the idea, to possess the beauty, which a great book contains, without staking his claim by pasting his bookplate inside the cover. Having a fine library doesn't prove that its owner has a mind enriched by books; it proves nothing more than that he, his father, or his wife, was rich enough to buy them.

There are three kinds of book owners. The first has all the standard sets and best-sellers—unread, untouched. (This deluded individual owns woodpulp and ink, not books.) The second has a great many books—a few of them read through, most of them dipped into, but all of them as clean and shiny as the day they were bought. (This person would probably like to make books his own, but is restrained by a false respect for their physical appearance.) The third has a few books or many—everyone of them dog-eared and dilapidated, shaken and loosened by continual use, marked and scribbled in from front to back. (This man owns books.)

Is it false respect, you may ask, to preserve intact and unblemished a beautifully printed book, an elegantly bound edition? Of course not. I'd no more scribble all over a first edition of *Paradise Lost* than I'd give my baby a set of crayons and an original Rembrandt! I wouldn't mark up a painting or a statue. Its soul, so to speak, is inseparable from its body. And the beauty of a rare edition or of a richly manufactured volume is like that of a painting or a statue.

But the soul of a book *can* be separated from its body. A book is more like the score of a piece of music than it is like a painting. No great musician confuses a symphony with the printed sheets of music. Arturo Toscanini reveres Brahms, but Toscanini's score of the C-minor Symphony is so thoroughly marked up that no one but the maestro himself can read it. The reason why a great conductor makes notations on his musical scores—marks them up again and again each time he returns to study them—is the reason why you should mark your books. If your respect for magnificent binding or typography gets in the way, buy yourself a cheap edition and pay your respects to the author.

Why is marking up a book indispensable to reading? First, it keeps you awake. (And I don't mean merely conscious; I mean wide awake.) In the second place, reading, if it is active, is thinking, and thinking tends to express itself in words, spoken or written. The marked book is usually the thought-through book. Finally, writing helps you remember the thoughts you had, or the thoughts the author expressed. Let me develop these three points.

If reading is to accomplish anything more than passing time, it must be active. You can't let your eyes glide across the lines of a book and come up with an understanding of what you have read. Now an ordinary piece of light fiction, like say, *Gone With the Wind*, doesn't require the most active kind of reading. The books you read for pleasure can be read in a state of relaxation, and nothing is lost. But a great book, rich in ideas and beauty, a book that raises and tries to answer great fundamental questions, demands the most active reading of which you are capable. You don't absorb the ideas of John Dewey the way you absorb the crooning of Mr. Vallee. You have to reach for them. That you cannot do while you're asleep.

If, when you've finished reading a book, the pages are filled with your notes, you know that you read actively. The most famous *active* reader of great books I know is President Hutchins, of the University of Chicago. He also has the hardest schedule of business activities of any man I know. He invariably reads with a pencil, and sometimes, when he picks up a book and pencil in the evening, he finds himself, instead of making intelligent notes, drawing what he calls "caviar factories" on the margins. When that happens, he puts the book down. He knows he's too tired to read, and he's just wasting time.

But, you may ask, why is writing necessary? Well, the physical act of writing, with your own hand, brings words and sentences more sharply before your mind and preserves them better in your memory. To set down your reaction to important words and sentences you have read, and the questions they have raised in your mind, is to preserve those reactions and sharpen those questions.

Even if you wrote on a scratch pad, and threw the paper away when you had finished writing, your grasp of the book would be surer. But you don't have to throw the paper away. The margins (top and bottom, as well as side), the end-papers, the very space between the lines, are all available. They aren't sacred. And, best of all, your marks and notes become an integral part of the book and stay there forever. You can pick up the book the following week or year, and there are all your points of agreement, disagreement, doubt, and inquiry. It's like resuming an interrupted conversation with the advantage of being able to pick up where you left off.

And that is exactly what reading a book should be: a conversation between you and the author. Presumably he knows more about the subject than you do; naturally, you'll have the proper humility as you approach him. But don't let anybody tell you that a reader is supposed to be solely on the receiving end. Understanding is a two-way operation; learning doesn't consist in being an empty receptacle. The learner has to question himself and question the teacher. He even has to argue with the teacher, once he understands what the teacher is saying. And marking a book is literally an expression of your differences, or agreements of opinion, with the author.

There are all kinds of devices for marking a book intelligently and fruitfully. Here's the way I do it:

1. *Underlining:* of major points, of important or forceful statements.

2. *Vertical lines at the margin:* to emphasize a statement already underlined.

3. *Star, asterisk, or other doo-dad at the margin:* to be used sparingly, to emphasize the ten or twenty most important statements in the book. (You may want to fold the bottom corner of each page on which you use such marks. It won't hurt the sturdy paper on which most modern books are printed, and you will be able to take the book off the shelf at any time and, by opening it at the folded corner page, refresh your recollection of the book.)

4. *Numbers in the margin:* to indicate the sequence of points the author makes in developing a single argument.

5. *Numbers of other pages in the margin:* to indicate where else in the book the author made points relevant to the point marked; to tie up the ideas in a book, which, though they may be separated by many pages, belong together.

6. *Circling of key words or phrases.*

7. *Writing in the margin, or at the top or bottom of the page, for the sake of:* recording questions (and perhaps answers) which a passage raised in your mind; reducing a complicated discussion to a simple statement; recording the sequence of major points right through the books. I use the end-papers at the back of the book to make a personal index of the author's points in the order of their appearance.

The front end-papers are, to me, the most important. Some people reserve them for a fancy bookplate. I reserve them for fancy thinking. After I have finished reading the book and making my personal index on the back end-papers, I turn to the front and try to outline the book, not page by page, or point by point (I've already done that at the back), but as an integrated structure, with a basic unity and an order of parts. This outline is, to me, the measure of my understanding of the work.

If you're a die-hard anti-book-marker, you may object that the margins, the space between the lines, and the end-papers don't give you room enough. All right. How about using a scratch pad slightly smaller than the page-size of the book—so that the edges of the sheets won't protrude? Make your index, outlines, and even your notes on the pad, and then insert these sheets permanently inside the front and back covers of the book.

Or, you may say that this business of marking books is going to slow up your reading. It probably will. That's one of the reasons for doing it. Most of us have been taken in by the notion that speed of reading is a measure of our intelligence. There is no such thing as the right speed for intelligent reading. Some things should be read quickly and effortlessly, and some should be read slowly and even laboriously. The sign of intelligence in reading is the ability to read different things differently according to their worth. In the case of good books, the point is not to see how many of them you can get through, but rather how many can get through you—how many you can make your own. A few friends are better than a thousand acquaintances. If this be your aim, as it should be, you will not be impatient if it takes more time and effort to read a great book than it does a newspaper.

You may have one final objection to marking books. You can't lend them to your friends because nobody else can read them without being distracted by your notes. Furthermore, you won't want to lend them because a marked copy is a kind of intellectual diary, and lending it is almost like giving your mind away.

If your friend wishes to read your *Plutarch's Lives*, Shakespeare, or *The Federalist Papers*, tell him gently but firmly to buy a copy. You will lend him your car or your coat—but your books are as much a part of you as your head or your heart.

33

"Learning to Read," from A *History of Reading*

Alberto Manguel

*Manguel explains that the teaching of reading in every
literate society involves an initiation of sorts, a rite of
passage. It is the way a child is introduced to the
heritage of family and faith. In medieval times, the
first teachers of reading to the children of aristocratic
families, both boys and girls, were mothers and nurses.*

In every literate society, learning to read is something of an initiation, a ritualized passage out of a state of dependency and rudimentary communication. The child learning to read is admitted into the communal memory by way of books, and thereby becomes acquainted with a common past which he or she renews, to a greater or lesser degree, in every reading. In medieval Jewish society, for instance, the ritual of learning to read was explicitly celebrated. On the Feast of Shavuot, when Moses received the Torah from the hands of God, the boy about to be initiated was wrapped in a prayer shawl and taken by his father to the teacher. The teacher sat the boy on his lap and showed him a slate on which were written the Hebrew alphabet, a passage from the Scriptures and the words "May the Torah be your occupation." The teacher read out every word and the child repeated it. Then the slate was covered with honey and the child licked it, thereby bodily assimilating the holy words. Also, biblical verses were written on peeled hard-boiled eggs and on honey cakes, which the child would eat after reading the verses out loud to the teacher.[1]

Though it is difficult to generalize over several centuries and across so many countries, in the Christian society of the late Middle Ages and the early Renaissance learning to read and write—outside the Church—was the almost exclusive privilege of the aristocracy and (after the thirteenth century) the upper bourgeoisie. Even though there were aristocrats and *grands bourgeois* who considered reading and writing menial tasks suitable only for poor clerics,[2] most boys and quite a few girls born to these classes were taught their letters very early. The child's nurse, if she could read, initiated the teaching, and for that reason had to be chosen with utmost care, since she was not only to provide milk but also to ensure correct speech and pronunciation.[3] The great Italian humanist scholar Leon Battista Alberti, writing between 1435 and 1444, noted that "the care of very young children is women's work, for nurses or the mother,"[4] and that at the earliest possible age they should be taught the alphabet. Children learned to read phonetically by repeating letters pointed out by their nurse or mother in a hornbook or alphabet sheet. (I myself was taught this way, by my nurse reading out to me the bold-type letters from an old English picture-book; I was made to repeat the sounds again and again.) The image of the teaching mother-figure was as common in Christian iconography as the female student was rare in depictions of the classroom. There are numerous representations of Mary holding a book in front of the Child Jesus, and of Anne teaching Mary, but neither Christ nor His Mother was depicted as learning to write or actually writing; it was the notion of Christ *reading* the Old Testament that was considered essential to make the continuity of the Scriptures explicit.

Quintilian, a first-century Roman lawyer from northern Spain who became the tutor of the Emperor Domitian's grand-nephews, wrote a twelve-volume pedagogical manual, the *Institutio oratoria*, which was highly influential throughout the Renaissance. In it, he advised: "Some hold that boys should not be taught to read till they are seven years old, that being the earliest age at which they can derive profit from instruction and endure the strain of learning. Those however who hold that a child's mind should not be allowed to lie fallow for a moment are wiser. Chrysippus, for instance, though he gives the nurses a three years' reign, still holds the formation of the child's mind on the best principles to be a part of their duties. Why again, since children are capable of moral training, should they not be capable of literary education?"[5]

After the letters had been learned, male teachers would be brought in as private tutors (if the family could afford them) for the boys, while the mother busied herself with the education of the girls. Even though, by the fifteenth century, most wealthy houses had the space, quiet and equipment to provide teaching at home, most scholars recommended that boys be educated away from the family, in the company of other boys; on the other hand, medieval moralists hotly debated the benefits of education—public or private—for girls. "It is not appropriate for girls to learn to read and write unless they wish to become nuns, since they might otherwise, coming of age, write or receive amorous missives,"[6] warned the nobleman Philippe de Novare, but several of his contemporaries disagreed. "Girls should learn to read in order to learn the true faith and protect themselves from the perils that menace their soul," argued the Chevalier de la Tour Landry.[7] Girls born in richer households were often sent to school to learn reading and writing, usually to prepare them for the convent. In the aristocratic households of Europe, it was possible to find women who were fully literate.

Notes

1. Israel Abrahams, *Jewish Life in the Middle Ages* (London, 1896).

2. I am grateful to Professor Roy Porter for this caveat.

3. Mateo Palmieri, *Della vita civile* (Bologna, 1944).

4. Leon Battista Alberti, *I Libridella famiglia*, ed. R. Romano and A. Tenenti (Turin, 1969).

5. Quintilian, *The Instituto Oratoria of Quintilian*, trans. H. E. Butler (Oxford 1920–22), line 12.

6. Quoted in Pierre Riche and Daniele Alexandre-Bidon, *L'Enfance au Moyen Age*. Catalogue of exhibition at the Bibliotheque Nationale, Paris, Oct. 26, 1994–Jan. 15, 1995 (Paris, 1995).

7. Ibid.

34

"Three Wise Guys: *Un Cuento de Navidad*/A Christmas Story"

Sandra Cisneros

*When a large, mysterious Christmas box arrives at
the home of the Gonzalez family, each family member
daydreams about what it might contain. You will be
as surprised as the family when you learn what is in
the box and what each family member does with the
contents. The story shows us the magic and power of
the unexpected.*

The big box came marked DO NOT OPEN TILL XMAS, but
the mama said not until the Day of the Three Kings. Not until
El Día de los Reyes, the 6th of January, do you hear? That is what
the mama said exactly, only she said it all in Spanish. Because in
Mexico where she was raised it is the custom for boys and girls to
receive their presents on January 6th, and not Christmas, even
though they were living on the Texas side of the river now. Not
until the 6th of January.

Yesterday the mama had risen in the dark same as always to
reheat the coffee in a tin saucepan and warm the breakfast tortillas.
The papa had gotten up coughing and spitting up the night, com-
plaining how the evening before the buzzing of the *chicharras* [cicadas,
which are cricket-like insects] had kept him from sleeping. By the
time the mama had the house smelling of oatmeal and cinnamon
the papa would be gone to the fields, the sun already tangled in the

trees and the *urracas* [magpies; birds having long, graduated tails and black-and-white plumage] screeching their rubber-screech cry. The boy Rubén and the girl Rosalinda would have to be shaken awake for school. The mama would go back to sleep before getting up again to the chores that were always waiting. That is how the world had been.

But today the big box had arrived. When the boy Rubén and the girl Rosalinda came home from school, it was already sitting in the living room in front of the television set that no longer worked. Who had put it there? Where had it come from? A box covered with red paper with green Christmas trees and a card on top that said: *Merry Christmas to the González Family. Frank, Earl, and Dwight Travis. P.S. DO NOT OPEN TILL XMAS.* That's all.

Two times the mama was made to come into the living room, first to explain to the children and later to their father how the brothers Travis had arrived in the blue pickup and how it had taken all three of those big men to lift the box off the back of the truck and bring it inside and how she had had to nod and say thank-you thank-you over and over because those were the only words she knew in English. Then the brothers Travis had nodded as well the way they always did when they came and brought the boxes of clothes or the turkey each November or the canned ham on Easter ever since the children had begun to earn high grades at the school where Dwight Travis was the principal.

But this year the Christmas box was bigger than usual. What could be in a box so big? The boy Rubén and the girl Rosalinda begged all afternoon to be allowed to open it, and that is when the mama had said the sixth of January, the Day of the Three Kings. Not a day sooner.

It seemed the weeks stretched themselves wider and wider since the arrival of the big box. The mama got used to sweeping around it because it was too heavy for her to push in a corner but since the television no longer worked ever since the afternoon the children had poured iced tea through the little grates in the back, it really didn't matter if it obstructed the view. Visitors that came inside the house were told and told again the story of how the box had arrived, and then each was made to guess what was inside.

It was the *comadre* [woman friend; also refers to a child's god-mother] Elodia who suggested over coffee one afternoon that the big box held a portable washing machine that could be rolled away when not in use, the kind she had seen in her Sears Roebuck catalogue. The mama said she hoped so because the wringer washer she had used for the last ten years had finally gotten tired and quit. These past few weeks she had had to boil all the clothes in the big pot she used for cooking the Christmas tamales. Yes. She hoped the big box was a portable washing machine. A washing machine, even a portable one, would be good.

But the neighborman Cayetano said, What foolishness, *comadre.* Can't you see the box is too small to hold a washing machine, even a portable one. Most likely God has heard your prayers and sent a new color t.v. With a good antenna you could catch all the Mexican soap operas, the neighborman said. You could distract yourself with the complicated troubles of the rich and then give thanks to God for the blessed simplicity of your poverty. A new t.v. would surely be the end to all your miseries.

Each night when the papa came home from the fields he would spread newspapers on the cot in the living room where the boy Rubén and the girl Rosalinda slept, and sit facing the big box in the center of the room. Each night he imagined the box held something different. The day before yesterday he guessed a new record player. Yesterday an ice chest filled with beer. Today the papa sat with his bottle of beer, fanning himself with a magazine and said in a voice as much a plea as a prophecy: air conditioner.

But the boy Rubén and the girl Rosalinda were sure the big box was filled with toys. They had even punctured a hole in one corner with a pencil when their mother was busy cooking, although they could see nothing inside but blackness.

Only the baby Gilberto remained uninterested in the contents of the big box and seemed each day more fascinated with the exterior of the box rather than the interior. One afternoon he tore off a fist-ful of paper which he was chewing when his mother swooped him up with one arm, rushed him to the kitchen sink, and forced him to swallow handfuls of lukewarm water in case the red dye of the wrapping paper might be poisonous.

When Christmas Eve finally came, the family González put on their good clothes and went to midnight mass. They came home to a house that smelled of tamales and *atole* [hot corn cereal], and everyone was allowed to open one present before going to sleep, but the big box was to remain untouched until the 6th of January.

On New Year's Eve the little house was filled with people, some related, some not, coming in and out. The friends of the papa came with bottles, and the mama set out a bowl of grapes to count off the New Year. That night the children did not sleep in the living room cot as they usually did because the living room was crowded with big-fannied ladies and fat-stomached men sashaying to the accordion music of the Midget Twins from McAllen. Instead the children fell asleep on a lump of handbags and crumpled suit jackets on top of the mama and the papa's bed, dreaming of the contents of the big box.

Finally the 5th of January. And the boy Rubén and the girl Rosalinda could hardly sleep. All night they whispered last minute wishes. The boy thought perhaps if the big box held a bicycle, he would be the first to ride it since he was the oldest. This made his sister cry until the mama had to yell from her bedroom on the other side of the plastic curtains, Be quiet or I'm going to give you each the stick, which sounds worse in Spanish than it does in English. Then no one said anything. After a very long time, long after they heard the mama's wheezed breathing and their papa's piped snoring, the children closed their eyes and remembered nothing.

The papa was already in the bathroom coughing up the night before from his throat when the *urracas* began their clownish chirp-

ing. The boy Rubén awoke and shook his sister. The mama frying
the potatoes and beans for breakfast nodded permission for the box
to be opened.

With a kitchen knife the boy Rubén cut a careful edge along the
top. The girl Rosalinda tore the Christmas wrapping with her fingernails. The papa and the mama lifted the cardboard flaps and
everyone peered inside to see what it was the brothers Travis had
brought them on the Day of the Three Kings.

There were layers of balled newspaper packed on top. When
these had been cleared away the boy Rubén looked inside. The girl
Rosalinda looked inside. The papa and the mama looked.

This is what they saw: the complete *Encyclopaedia Britannica
Junior,* twenty-four volumes in red imitation leather with gold-
embossed letters beginning with volume 1, Aar-Bel, and ending
with volume 24, Yel-Zyn. The girl Rosalinda let out a sad cry as if
her hair was going to be cut again. The boy Rubén pulled out volume 4, Ded-Fem. There were many pictures. The papa flipped
through volume 22, but because he could not read English words,
simply put the book back and grunted, What can we do with this?
No one said anything and shortly after, the screen door slammed.

Only the mama knew what to do with the contents of the big
box. She withdrew volumes 6, 7, and 8, marched off to the dinette
set in the kitchen, placed two on Rosalinda's chair so she could better reach the table, and put one underneath the plant stand that
danced.

When the boy and the girl returned from school that day they
found the books stacked into squat pillars against one living room
wall and a board placed on top. On this were arranged several plastic doilies and framed family photographs. The rest of the volumes
the baby Gilberto was playing with, and he was already rubbing his
sore gums along the corners of volume 14.

The girl Rosalinda also grew interested in the books. She took
out her colored pencils and painted blue on the lids of all the illustrations of women and with a red pencil dipped in spit she painted

their lips and fingernails red-red. After a couple of days when all the pictures of women had been colored in this manner, she began to cut out some of the prettier pictures and paste them on loose-leaf paper.

One volume suffered from being exposed to the rain when the papa improvised a hat during a sudden shower. He forgot it on the hood of the car when he drove off. When the children came home from school they set it on the porch to dry. But the pages puffed up and became so fat, the book was impossible to close.

Only the boy Rubén refused to touch the books. For several days he avoided the principal because he didn't know what to say in case Mr. Travis were to ask how they were enjoying the Christmas present.

On the Saturday after New Year's the mama and the papa went into town for groceries and left the boy in charge of watching his sister and baby brother. The girl Rosalinda was stacking books into spiral staircases and making her paper dolls descend them in a fancy manner.

Perhaps the boy Rubén would not have bothered to open the volume left on the kitchen table if he had not seen his mother wedge her name-day [the church feast day of the saint after whom one is named] corsage in its pages. On the page where the mama's carnation lay pressed between two pieces of kleenex was a picture of a dog in a space ship. FIRST DOG IN SPACE the caption said. The boy turned to another page and read where cashews came from. And then about Bengal tigers. And about clouds. All afternoon the boy read, even after the mama and the papa came home. Even after the sun set until the mama said time to sleep and put the light out.

In their bed on the other side of the plastic curtain the mama and the papa slept. Across from them in the crib slept the baby Gilberto. The girl Rosalinda slept on her end of the cot. But the boy Rubén watched the night sky turn from violet. To blue. To grey. And then from grey. To blue. To violet once again.

35

"The New Case for Latin"

Mike Eskenazi

This selection is about the effects of studying Latin in order to help students better understand English. Because about 65 percent of English words have Latin roots, students who learn the Latin roots will more easily discern word meaning than those who do not. According to the author, this approach is useful in helping students improve their reading.

Amy High is decked out in the traditional pink dress and golden stole of ancient Rome. She bursts into a third-grade classroom and greets her students: "*Salvete, omnes!*" (Hello, everyone!) The kids respond in kind, and soon they are studying derivatives. "How many people are in a duet?" High asks. All the kids know the answer, and when she asks how they know, a boy responds, "Because *duo* is 'two' in Latin." High replies, "*Plaudite!*" and the 14 kids erupt in applause. They learn the Latin root *later*, or side, and construct such English words as bilateral and quadrilateral. "Latin's going to open up so many doors for you," High says. "You're going to be able to figure out the meaning of words you've never seen before."

High teaches at Providence Elementary School in Fairfax City, Va., which has a lot riding on the success of her efforts. As part of Virginia's high-stakes testing program, schools that don't boost their scores by the year 2007 could lose state funding. So Fairfax City, just 18 miles southwest of the White House, has upgraded its two crumbling elementary schools with new high-tech television studios, computer labs and one very old feature—mandatory Latin.

Here lies one of the more counterintuitive developments of the standardized-testing movement. Though some critics complain that teachers are forced to dumb down their lessons and "teach to the test," some schools are offering more challenging course work as a way of engaging students. In the past three years, scores of elementary schools in high-stakes testing states such as Texas, Virginia and Massachusetts have added Latin programs. Says Allen Griffith, a member of the Fairfax City school board: "If we're trying to improve English skills, teaching Latin is an awfully effective, proved method."

This is not your father's Latin, which was taught to élite college-bound high schoolers and drilled into them through memorization. Its tedium and perceived irrelevance almost drove Latin from public schools. Today's growth in elementary school Latin has been spurred by new, interactive oral curriculums, enlivened by lessons in Roman mythology and culture. "One thing that makes it engaging for kids is the goofy fun of investigating these guys in togas," says Marion Polsky, author of First Latin: A Language Discovery Program, the textbook used in Fairfax City.

Latin enthusiasts believe that if young students learn word roots, they will be able to decipher unfamiliar words. (By some estimates, 65% of all English words have Latin roots.) Latin is an almost purely phonetic language. There are no silent letters, and each letter represents a single sound. That makes it useful in teaching reading. And once kids master the grammatical structure of Latin—which is simple, logical and consistent—they will more easily grasp the many grammatical exceptions in English.

In the 1970s and '80s, the U.S. government funded Latin classes in underperforming urban school districts. The results were dramatic. Children who were given a full year of Latin performed five months to a year ahead of control groups in reading comprehension and vocabulary. The Latin students also showed outsize gains in math, history and geography. But Congress cut the funding, and nearly all the districts discontinued Latin.

Some curriculum experts have examined the evidence and still favor modern languages instead of Latin. John Chubb, chief executive of the Edison charter schools, said the company decided to make Spanish, not Latin, mandatory in its elementary schools because "we want our kids to be socialized to the outside world."

Still, Griffith, the Fairfax City schoolboard member, believes that "so far, the Latin looks like a good investment." He took encouragement from the confident smiles of Amy High's students each time they correctly responded to a question. "They're so receptive," says High. "They don't even know they're learning."

Bona Fide Glossary

- ALTER EGO Second self
- ANTEBELLUM Before the war
- BONA FIDE In good faith
- CARPE DIEM Seize the day
- CAVEAT EMPTOR Let the buyer beware
- CURRICULUM VITAE The course of one's life
- E PLURIBUS UNUM Out of many, one
- MODUS OPERANDI (M.O.) Method of operating
- PERSONA NON GRATA An unwelcome person
- QUID PRO QUO Something (given or received) for something
- SEMPER UBI SUB UBI Always wear underwear
- VOX POPULI Voice of the people

36

"No Words," from *Wild Country:*
Outdoor Poems for Young People

David Harrison

*Harrison shares his feelings that words are
"poor shabby symbols at best." He leads us to
contemplate what a world would be like
without words, without reading, without
language.*

No words
are as big as a mountain,
blue as a summer sky,
flickering quick
as a hummingbird's wing,
bright as a butterfly.

No words
taste as sweet as wild honey,
glow like a setting sun,
howl at the moon
like wolves in the night,
leap like a stag on the run.

No words
can paint pictures of nature,

they're poor shabby symbols at best
that only remind us
that beauty surrounds us,
the heart must supply the rest.

37

"Teaching People to Hate Literature"

Matthew S.

*Matthew, a high school student, attacks elementary
and secondary teachers for destroying young people's
love of reading by teaching too much form and
analysis of literature. He believes that books should
be taught free of structured study in order to sustain
the emotional appeal of the reading that engages
students in the first place.*

Why can't Americans read? Today, it seems that adult society,
with the exception of a small, elite group, reads next to
nothing. Relatively few people read novels, and almost no one reads
poetry. Why is it that love of reading isn't widespread? It is evident
that people are not born with an aversion to reading. Young children love poetry and nursery rhymes, and they beg for bedtime
stories. Yet something happens between elementary school and
adulthood that kills our natural love of the written word. I believe
that the major force working against a love of literature is, ironi-
cally, middle and high school English classes.

The first flaw in the secondary school literature programs lies in
book selection. Often those who select the books are so concerned
with whether the book in question is important enough, classic
enough, relevant enough, fits in with the theme of the year, and is
part of the so-called literary canon, that they lose sight of the fact

that reading is supposed to be a pleasurable experience. Sometimes the books are selected so poorly that kids are driven away, especially if they are just starting to read serious novels. But in my opinion, the real, fundamental flaw lies not in what books are chosen, but in how they are taught.

Literature classes seem to go out of their way to force children to hate reading. All one has to do to realize this is to look at the way books are taught. One is not able to simply read a book and absorb it. Instead, students dissect books and analyze them, effectively ripping the novel to shreds. I still remember my seventh grade English teacher insisting that we had to "read with our pencils," methodically underlining important or symbolic passages. Reading with a pencil turned literature into drudgery.

Surely authors do not write books so readers can dissect every sentence and analyze every comma. Teaching English this way is like a couple constantly discussing the meaning of their relationship. The communication gets lost in the words. A book is a whole, and should be read as such. The whole is greater than the sum of its parts.

Does this mean that the study of the structure of literature has no place in education? Of course not. For some who will specialize in literature, this is appropriate at some point after high school, just as some art students go on to analyze brush strokes and some musicians study music theory. However, in a high school literature course, the most important objective to be gained is a love of reading. Moreover, the current method of teaching is failing to impart more than the most basic skills. According to a 1989 study, only about five percent of seventeen-year-olds in the United States could read at the advanced level, which the study defined as being able to understand the links between ideas even when those links are not explicitly stated and to make appropriate generalizations even when the texts lack clear introductions or explanations. Less than 40 percent could read at the adept level, defined as being able to find, understand, summarize and explain relatively complicated literary and informational material.

What can be done about the serious problems in our system of teaching literature? Obviously we can't stop teaching. What we must do is realize that the aim of literature is to have some sort of emotional impact on the reader. Sentence structure or parallel construction are only tools. Books should be taught through open discussion and not through structured study. I have always found that I enjoy books much more when I read them on my own. If one walks away from a book having disliked the experience of reading and studying it, then it matters little how accurately the book was analyzed; the whole experience was wasted.

I would argue that we must rethink the objectives and methods of teaching secondary school literature. Good books speak for themselves, and we shouldn't try too hard to pull them apart to find the meaning. If the meaning is there, it will find us. As Archibald MacLeish wrote in his poem "Ars Poetica," "A poem should not mean but be." He does not mean that poems have no meaning, but that they must be understood on their own terms, not analyzed. Teachers and fellow students can help guide us and share the experience, but too much structured study can destroy the pleasure of reading. As Mark Twain wrote in the humorous, but very significant introduction to his masterpiece, Huckleberry Finn: "Persons attempting to find a motive in this narrative will be prosecuted; persons attempting to find a moral in it will be banished; persons attempting to find a plot in it will be shot."

38

"Team Xerox"

Chris Taylor

*This selection addresses the development of new
visions of reading so that we can read and process
large amounts of information in less time by altering
the way the material is presented to us and changing
our reading habits. Be prepared to speculate on new
ways of reading what the writer describes as "muta-
tions of the book."*

Take a look at what your eyes are doing right now. It's known as
saccadic jumping—the way they skip across the page from left
to right before some unseen hand comes in and pushes them to the
start of the next line, like the ball on an old typewriter. It's something you've done your whole life. But is it really the most efficient
way to read?

Now imagine this: you're sitting at a computer equipped with a
steering wheel, gas pedal, brake and stick shift. Words appear on the
screen at a speed you determine by applying the pedals. Your eyes
don't waste time with saccadic jumps, since there's never more than
one word on the screen at a time. The wheel steers you between
chapters; the stick shift takes you to the next book. Before you know
it, your brain has become some kind of jet-powered Maserati. Reading regular text, you're considered fleet of eye if you hit 400 words

a minute; on this device, known as the Speeder Reader, test subjects have been known to manage 2,000 words a minute.

Which doesn't mean we're all going to spend the 21st century treating books like NASCAR racetracks. But as an effective tool for cramming large chunks of information (the technology it is based on is already a big hit with law students), Speeder Reader is proof positive that we also don't have to treat books like slabs of paper that sit on shelves anymore. Printed text, which has remained basically unchanged since Gutenberg first got his fingers inky, is about to bloom into a thousand different forms. The one you use will increasingly depend on what you need to use it for. "The tyranny of the static book is over," says Rich Gold, head of the Research on Experimental Documents (RED) team at Xerox PARC. "The digital revolution can incorporate radical new visions of reading."

Reinventing the book? It's not the kind of thing you'd expect to find preoccupying even the most eccentric inventor's mind. Yet Xerox PARC (it stands for Palo Alto Research Center) is the kind of place that prides itself on overturning assumptions. For one, there are no lone nuts tinkering away in silent labs. Teamwork takes priority here—and as history suggests, there's nothing more powerful than the feedback effect of inventors riffing off one another's work.

The PARC has a pretty good track record when it comes to radical new visions, even if its record of holding onto them has been spotty at best. The mouse, the GUI (graphical user interface, like Windows) and arguably the PC itself were all born in this hothouse of Silicon Valley R. and D.; they ended up making a lot of money for Apple and Microsoft. Xerox has got a lot of prestige but little cash out of the PARC, which is why the beleaguered copier giant intimated in October [2000] that it would put its crown jewel up for sale to help stem billion-dollar losses.

While its future ownership is in doubt, the buttoned-down brain trust at PARC has lost none of the anything-goes enthusiasm that made it famous in the first place. It's a place where experts from entirely different academic disciplines mind-meld furiously, then run off in pursuit of the most challenging technological problems they can come up with. And right now, at the dawn of the Internet age, PARC scientists are most motivated by the question of how we digest our increasingly bloated diet of data. After all, they say, your total potential reading matter increased by a factor of 10,000 during the 1990s. "In a world where information is abundant, the scarce resource is attention," says Stu Card of PARC's User Interface research team. "That's what we're trying to do—manage user attention."

Both Gold and Card have this aim in mind, but there the similarities end. Gold is deeply tanned, ponytailed and fast talking, with a background in experimental music and toy design. His group has spent the past couple of years dreaming up utterly outlandish text-display inventions like Speeder Reader. There's the Tilty Table, a vast and thin computer screen on shock absorbers that you tilt in any direction to scroll through a document that would in real life be 30 ft. across; Listen Reader, which uses tiny embedded computer chips to produce different ambient sounds on each page of a children's book; and the Reading-Eye Dog, a robotic pet that uses a text-to-voice synthesizer to read out anything you care to put in front of it (making it fetch the paper as well as read it to you may take a little while longer).

Card, by contrast, is a soft-spoken, slightly geeky-looking psychologist and computer scientist; his group is involved in the more practical, down-to-earth business of making the Web more readable. He uses the jargon of Internet ecology, talking about the way we "forage" for information and hunt its "scent" to produce a balanced "diet." But that doesn't make his tools and results any less gee-whiz than Gold's. Step into Card's lab, and he will show you the device he uses on his test subjects, a metal headpiece with little cameras positioned in front of each eye. This scary-looking machine records your saccadic jumps while you hunt for information, and notes how long it takes for your pupils to dilate (that is, when you've found the particular scent you're looking for). His conclusion: "People tend to spend a lot more time skimming than reading."

You might think this would be a point in favor of hypertext links, those ubiquitous wormholes of the Web. Not so, says Card's team: its research shows the average user gets confused by blue underlined words, and that these links too often fail to communicate exactly where they're taking you. So what's the solution? Ask Card, and he will point to the screen shot of an enormous multi-sided shape his team jokingly refers to as the Death Star.

It's actually called the Perspective Wall, and it lets you navigate hundreds of Web pages at a time without having to lose sight of any of them. Move to the one you want, and it enlarges while the others shrink. With each page color coded for relevance, it's a skimmer's dream—and the online search result of the future. "Bar charts weren't invented 250 years ago," says Peter Pirolli, Card's fellow psychologist. "Now we take them for granted. The same thing is happening with the computer. We're becoming more visual." And therefore less literate? "It's a different kind of literate culture," Pirolli insists.

Skimming the Surface

Gold's RED team seems to have reached the same conclusion: it's O.K. to skim, and it's O.K. to read pictures instead of text. Its Hyperbolic Reader (based on the hyperbolic tree, a Xerox PARC invention) tells a children's story in Perspective Wall style. Cartoons and speech bubbles grow large as you move a joystick over them, then shrink as you turn to another part of the story's tree. In Fluid Fiction (also created with PARC software), another children's story is told in just 24 sentences. But touch the end of any sentence, and the text parts, revealing a new set of sentence endings. Touch one, and you're down to the story's third layer. The device literally teaches kids to read between the lines.

But in all these inventions and the philosophy behind them, it's hard not to get a sobering sense of the impending death of traditional, text-based linear narrative. Will generations to come ever know the delights of picking up a good book and reading it from start to finish? Or will they rather skim through it on their tablet PCs, Speeder Reading what the computer has predetermined to be the best bits based on their previous preferences, choosing alternative endings, letting the robot dog finish it for them?

On the other hand, we should be glad they're reading at all. The RED team's inventions were a huge hit with the thousands of kids who packed the San Jose, Calif., Tech Museum of Innovation from March to October this year; so much so that the exhibit will tour the country in 2001. "Kids are very accepting of these new forms of reading," says RED researcher Maribeth Back. "We've made the book more responsive, in the same way other electronic appliances they know are. The book form we know starts to look less and less sacred."

Not that those lumps of paper on our shelves have been sacred in this form for very long. It's less than 200 years since the arrival of the novel, and less than 100 since the average best seller came with illustrations. The brave new world of reading under construction at Xerox PARC may be only the latest step in the book's evolution. The more forms it can mutate into, the more likely it is that one of those forms will survive in an age of intensive information foraging and visual literacy. And if that form happens to be Speeder Reader—well, at least you'll have fun teaching your grandchildren how to do saccadic jumps.

39

"Private Reading,"
from A History of Reading

Alberto Manguel

*A relationship exists between what we read and where
and when we read it. Some books are meant to be
read while sitting at a desk, while others require a
comfortable chair. Some are for reading in bed just
before sleep, while others lend themselves to a sunny
afternoon at the beach. All of us have our preferences. This selection leaves us to contemplate our
own requirements.*

I too read in bed. In the long succession of beds in which I spent
the nights of my childhood, in strange hotel rooms where the
lights of passing cars swept eerily across the ceiling, in houses whose
smells and sounds were unfamiliar to me, in summer cottages sticky
with sea spray or where the mountain air was so dry that a steaming basin of eucalyptus water was placed by my side to help me
breathe, the combination of bed and book granted me a sort of
home which I knew I could go back to, night after night, under
whichever skies. No one would call out and ask me to do this or
that; my body needed nothing, immobile under the sheets. What
took place, took place in the book, and I was the story's teller. Life
happened because I turned the pages. I don't think I can remember
a greater *comprehensive* joy than that of coming to the few last pages
and setting the book down, so that the end would not take place

until at least tomorrow, and sinking back into my pillow with the sense of having actually stopped time.

I knew that not every book was suitable for reading in bed. Detective stories and tales of the supernatural were most likely to grant me a peaceful sleep. For Colette, *Les Misérables*, with its streets and forests, flights down dark sewers and across battling barricades, was the perfect book for the quiet of the bedroom. W. H. Auden agreed. He suggested that the book one reads should somehow be at odds with the place in which it's read. "I can't read Jefferies or the Wiltshire Downs," he complained, "nor browse on limericks in a smoking room." This may be true; there may be a sense of redundancy in exploring on the page a world similar to the one surrounding us at the very moment of reading. I think of André Gide reading Boileau as he was being ferried down the Congo, and the counterpoint between the lush, disorderly vegetation and the chiselled, formal seventeenth-century verse seems exactly right.

But, as Colette discovered, not only do certain books demand a contrast between their contents and their surroundings; some books seem to demand particular *positions* for reading, postures of the reader's body that in turn require reading-places appropriate to those postures. (For instance, she wasn't able to read Michelet's *Histoire de France* until she found herself curled up in her father's armchair with Fanchette, "that most intelligent of cats.") Often the pleasure derived from reading largely depends on the bodily comfort of the reader.

"I have sought for happiness everywhere," confessed Thomas à Kempis, early in the fifteenth century, "but I have found it nowhere except in a little corner with a little book." But which little corner? And which little book? Whether we first choose the book and then an appropriate corner, or first find the corner and then decide what book will suit the corner's mood, there is no doubt that the act of reading in time requires a corresponding act of reading in place, and the relationship between the two acts is inextricable. There are books I read in armchairs, and there are books I read at desks; there are books I read in subways, on streetcars and on buses. I find that books read in trains have something of the quality of books read in armchairs, perhaps because in both I can easily abstract myself from my surroundings. "The best time for reading a good stylish story," said the English novelist Alan Sillitoe, "is in fact when one is on a train travelling alone. With strangers roundabout, and unfamiliar scenery passing by the window (at which you glance now and again) the endearing and convoluted life coming out of the pages possesses its own peculiar and imprinting effects." Books read in a public library never have the same flavor as books read in the attic or the kitchen. In 1374, King Edward III paid £66 13s 4d for a book of romances "to be kept in his bedchamber," where he obviously thought such a book should be read. In the twelfth-century *Life of Saint Gregory*, the toilet is described as "a retiring place where tablets can be read without interruption." Henry Miller agreed: "All my good reading was done in the toilet," he once confessed. "There are passages of *Ulysses* which can be read only in the toilet—if one wants to extract the full flavor of their content." In fact, the little room "destined for a more special and vulgar use" was for Marcel Proust a place "for all my occupations which required an inviolable solitude: reading, reverie, tears and sensual pleasure."

The epicurean Omar Khayyam recommended reading verse out-doors under a bough; centuries later, the punctilious Sainte-Beuve advised reading the *Memoirs* of Mme de Staël "under November's trees." "My custom," wrote Shelley, "is to undress, and sit on the rocks, reading Herodotus, until the perspiration has subsided." But not everyone is capable of reading under an open sky. "I seldom read on beaches or in gardens," confessed Marguerite Duras. "You can't read by two lights at once, the light of day and the light of the book. You should read by electric light, the room in shadow, and only the page lit up."

One can transform a place by reading in it. During the summer holidays, Proust would sneak back into the dining-room once the rest of the family had left on its morning walk, confident that his only companions, "very respectful of reading," would be "the painted plates hung on the wall, the calendar where yesterday's page had been freshly torn away, the clock and the hearth, who speak without expecting an answer and whose babble, unlike human words, does not attempt to replace the sense of the words you are reading with another, different sense." Two full hours of bliss before the cook would appear, "far too early, to lay the table; and if at least she had laid it without speaking! But she felt obliged to say, 'You can't be comfortable like that; and if I brought you a desk?' And just by having to answer, 'No, thank you very much,' one was forced to come to a full stop and bring back from far away one's voice, which, hidden behind the lips, repeated soundlessly, and very fast, all the words read by the eyes; one had to bring one's voice to a halt, bring it into the open and, in order to say properly, 'No, thank you very much,' give it an everyday appearance, an answering intonation which it had lost." Only much later—at night, well after dinner—and when there were but a few pages of the book left to read, would he relight his candle, risking punishment if discovered, and insomnia, because once the book was finished, the passion with which he had followed the plot and its heroes would make it impossible for him to sleep, and he'd pace the room or lie breathlessly, wishing for the story to continue, or wishing to know at least something more about the characters he had loved so well.

Part IV

Breaking Codes

Selections reflect our need to navigate unfamiliar types of texts.

40

"Susan Schulter," from *Speaking of Reading*

Susan Schulter

*For Schulter, blind since birth, books provide an
important way of experiencing the world. She writes,
"Reading is my photography. When I read, I feel the
way I imagine people feel when they look at pictures.
I become transported to wherever it is that I'm reading about. Reading is my bridge between me and
everywhere."*

I had a very rich childhood. I was read to and sung to a zillion
times. My mother constantly read bedtime stories to us, even
news articles that pertained to children. One of my first experiences
with literacy was when we wrote a letter to Santa Claus before I
could actually write. I told my mother what I wanted to say and she
wrote it down. Around that same period, my mother took me and
my siblings to the library, where we got library cards. It was a rainy
day and I remember feeling the sacredness of the library because we
whispered. We came home and I told my father about it.

We had lots of books around the house and general encyclopedias, *National Geographic*, and *Sunset*—reading material that invited
discovery. My mother was very neat, but there was always a book
open somewhere. She'd say, "That's OK, a book should be open
because it is asking you to enter it."

I went to a preschool for children with visual impairments. It is the only special school I went to because after that I was mainstreamed in public schools. At the preschool, I had my first introduction to braille. We learned to write our own names on a little Dyno labeler. I remember that day—I held the little plastic with the tape on the back in my hand and I went over and over it saying, "That's me!"

When I was in kindergarten, I began receiving talking books for the blind. There's a whole studio in the Library of Congress that records books on disc, record, and tape for people who can't see. Those books gave me my first introduction to E. B. White's *Stuart Little* and *Charlotte's Web*—they were talking books read by a male narrator. Later, in second grade, when my teacher was reading *Charlotte's Web*, I had some difficulty because she didn't voice things the way he had. I already had certain characterizations in mind, and had to make adjustments because her reading was different. Only later did I realize I could put my own voice to those characters.

So my earliest reading experiences were quite auditory, then they became tactile, especially in the first grade. When I went to public schools we had a resource program for the ten blind youngsters in the district. We had a special resource teacher who taught us our braille skills as well as phonics and math—everything our peers were learning, but in braille. We spent most of our day with her. Then, in the mainstream classroom, she would provide the materials in braille, we would do our work in braille, and she would transcribe it.

In the sixth grade I read a book called *Road to Volograd* about a Hindu boy in India whose younger sister is going blind. He walks her from their village all the way to the city of Vogra to see a doctor there. The book is full of the exotic. They go down a well to sleep, then wake up because they hear a cobra scratching its scales over the rocks as it moves. He talks about wrapping food up in banana leaves and about the smell of elephants and burning cow dung. All that was so foreign to my experience, yet I had had experiences with bananas, if not banana leaves, and I knew what other manure smells like when it's burning, so I made the connections. As long as the experience was sensory, I could make a connection. I once petted an elephant at a zoo, and I once heard an elephant scream at the circus, so when I read that book, I was able to connect with it. If I have to make up too much, I usually don't like the book. But then, that's probably true for anybody.

There's a passage in *The Wind in the Willows* where the mole, who has been away from home for about a year, is out on a winter day running with the rat, and all of a sudden he falls over on his haunches and says, "Oh no, oh dear, oh dear." He starts sobbing and crying. He says, "It's my home. I smell it." They go tunneling around under the snow and find his home. I've had that experience myself. I went to church one time and the smell of the wood was identical to the smell of a church that was near a cabin we used to go to when I was a little girl. It was the smell of sun on boards and firewood smoke. I walked into that church and instantly remembered that passage from *The Wind in the Willows*, and I said, "Yeah, that's what smell does."

Science fiction is all the same unless there is something human, universal, about what's happening to a character. I liked Robert Heinlein's *Stranger in a Strange Land* because Valentine Michael Smith wanted to learn how to love—he wanted to learn what sexual and sensual and emotional closeness was. There was a funny word for that, grocking. It was a human experience I could relate to. There's also a Ray Bradbury story, "All Summer in a Day," about a little girl on the planet Venus, where it rains all the time except for once every seven years when the sun comes out. She remembers the sun from when she lived on Earth, so she tells her class how much they are going to love it. She talks about jungles and steam and the smell of wet plants and how they feel springing under your feet. These are things I know. The other children don't believe her, so they lock her in the school linen closet. The sun comes out and they all go outside to play and forget her. Then it starts to rain again and they remember her and let her out.

I also very much like the way language sounds. That's why I like to read and write poetry. The connection between poetry and music is constantly going on for me. Poetry goes back to music. The first poetry I remember well is A Child's Garden of Verses by Robert Louis Stevenson. I had a recording of it when I was little. I really liked the way the lines rhymed with each other. I can still remember falling in love with the sound of Robert Frost's reading voice because he sounded like my grandfather. One of my school projects as a child was taking Frost's poem, "Birches," and gathering little branches from the birch trees in the front yard and setting them up in Styrofoam and varnishing them so they would look snowed on. To me all this was reading, all of it was making books come alive for me.

When I read, I hear it and I see it in braille. When I read a book, like Paradise Lost, for instance, I can see the way the dots look in my head. It's a tactile image, but it's there. I use the word see because it's so common. Now I also have a reading machine which runs like a scanner. It provides everything in auditory feedback. I find I remember text auditorily in chunks, and I can reconstruct a whole block at a time, whereas the documents I experience in braille I remember more linearly, sentence by sentence.

I also find that I'm a very bad speller, although I'm getting better. This has to do with being an auditory reader. I have a braille computer that I can connect to the scanner which can give me a braille readout of anything I'm listening to, and I find that if I see a word with my fingertips, I remember how to spell it. It has a completely different character than if I hear it. I can't say I like one form better than the other—I like putting them together.

I teach freshman composition courses. My students type their papers and my optical scanner scans them and reads the papers aloud to me. I listen to the paper once through first from beginning to end, trying not to let myself stop along the way. I jot down my overall impressions of the content on my little braille word processor. Then I listen through again, stopping quite a bit to write down specific notes on certain sentences that read ungrammatically. The scanner mispronounces misspelled words, so I can catch them too. Sometimes I copy down whole sentences to decide what kind of recommendation to make, a transition that doesn't seem to be working, or paragraphing that needs work. All of this is rather tedious. Sighted instructors would probably circle or underline or write arrows and notes. Next I must decide how I want to respond to that paper. I usually compose a letter in response to the student on my word processor. My students get their own work back and my letter stapled to it rather than read marks on their paper. They have told me they like their own text coming back untarnished.

Before I got the scanner, they taped their papers and I listened to the tapes, and spoke my remarks back into the tape. The students with very good auditory skills like that, but the more visual students prefer the letter. If the students do handwritten work in class, I have my teaching assistant read the papers to me and I tell her what I want her to write on the paper.

I remember the names of the authors and the characters of the books I've read quite well. It's my math, it's my orientation pattern. It helps me know where I am in time and space to be able to remember them all. I get a real warm pleasure when I recall books I have read, like seeing somebody that I love after I haven't seen her or him for a few years. I get a sense of belonging when I can do that. It's a nice reminder that there really was a past, and that there is a sense of the future. It's a wonderful, grounding experience to have a record, a documentation that lives have existed before our own. I've always thought that writing and music have the power to say, "Yes, this confirms it—so-and-so was here before." I need that connection. I think it would be frightening to live only in the present.

41

"Important: Read This First"

Frank Cammuso, Hart Seely

*The authors make a witty and humorous presentation
on writing a manual on how to read a book.*

*T*ime Warner Trade Publishing is paying John F. Welch Jr., the chair-
man of the General Electric Company, $7.1 million for the rights
to his story. This continues G.E.'s long tradition of bringing good literature to life.

Congratulations on your purchase of the most reliable and
dependable text appliance on the market today, the Portable John F.
Welch Jr. Autobiography System (Model GE-TW-2000A). Please
read instructions carefully before attempting to use this product.
(Spanish Quick-Use Guide is included. *Guía para rápida consulta en
español está incluido.*)

Section 1. Installation

After unpacking unit, make sure all parts are present. (See Fig. 1.)

Item	Quantity
(a) 8.5 × 7 Front Panel (BB-W3049)	1
(b) 8.5 × 7 Rear Panel (BB-W3094)	1

(c) 8.5 × 21 Exterior Dust Protection Display
Sheath (BB-W30941)   1

(d) 8.5 × 7 Interior Print Text Sheets (BB-W4000-
BB-W4434)   434

If any part is missing or damaged, contact an authorized G.E./
Time Warner service outlet or a trained G.E./Time Warner service
technician. Do not attempt to remove panel and repair text your-
self. CAUTION: USE OF UNAUTHORIZED REPLACEMENT
TEXT MAY CAUSE BLURRED RECEPTION, SHOCK OR
LIBEL SUIT.

For optimum performance, avoid use outside during lightning
storms or while operating a motor vehicle, power tool or cutting
instrument. Store unit away from excessive water or moisture, such
as in a kitchen sink or bathtub. If exposed to rain or moisture, leave
unit OPEN and let dry. DO NOT PLACE IN EXTREME HEAT.

NOTE: IF UNIT IS UNUSED FOR AN EXTENDED PERIOD
OF TIME, USER MAY EXPERIENCE LOSS OF INTEREST.

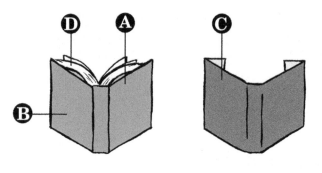

Fig. 1   ILLUSTRATIONS BY FRANK CAMMUSO

Section 2. Manual Configuration

(a) After inspection of parts (Section 1), locate Front Panel (BB-
W3049) by holding center spinal quoin with both hands, position-

ing flat surface of Exterior Dust Protection Display Sheath (BB-W30941) so as to face user squarely, approximately 14–18 inches from eyes. (See Fig. 2.) CAUTION: DO NOT JAB EDGES OR CORNERS OF UNIT INTO EYES OR MOUTH. (FIRST AID: EYES—Rinse with water for 15 minutes. IF SWALLOWED— Harmful or fatal. Contact physician immediately.)

(b) Holding base of unit with unruffled edge to the left, rotate until the following text appears:

By John F. Welch Jr.

(NOTE: YOU MAY RECEIVE THIS ERROR MESSAGE

By John F. Welch Jr.

IF SO, CONTINUE ROTATING UNTIL PROPER TEXT APPEARS.)

You have configured the Front Panel (BB-W3049). You are now ready to operate!

CORRECT

INCORRECT

Fig. 2

Section 3. Manual Operation

(a) Holding unit securely, gently pry unhinged edge (right side) of Front Panel (BB-W3049) upward, lifting from body assembly and pulling in right-to-left motion, so as to form a V-shape (or inverted A without center bar).

(b) Holding base of unit, repeat (a) with Interior Print Text Sheet No. 1 (BB-W4000).

(c) Repeat in numerical (preferred) sequence. (For BROWSE and RANDOM MODE functions, see Page 49 of this manual.)

Section 4. Mobility Operation (for G.E. Employees and Contractors)

(a) Mount unit on a flat surface, such as a coffee table or desktop, in area of high visibility.

(b) Refer to unit as "best damn book I ever read!"

(c) Repeat (b) as needed. (For advanced users, consult Supplemental Manual (BB-W4), "Getting the Most From This Product.")

Section 5. Trouble-Shooting

Before requesting service on this unit, check the list below for a possible cause of the problem you are experiencing. Some simple checks or a minor adjustment on your part may restore proper operation.

Problem: All the words are upside down and backward.

Solution: Reconfiguration required. (See Section 2.)

Problem: I don't know what is happening in the story.

Solution: Return to last chapter you can remember.

Problem: Unit closes by itself.

Solution: With unit in "open" position (splayed A-shape), sit or stand on it squarely for 15–30 seconds until loud "crack" is heard. (See Fig. 3.)

Fig. 3

(If problem persists, consider purchasing compatible Portable Book Marking Device GE-TW-2000B.)

Problem: I'm reading but don't hear anything.

Solution: See Page 56, "Oral and/or Silent Text Processing."

Problem: I have no more pages to turn.

Solution: Congratulations. You finished. Fortunately, the Portable John F. Welch Jr. Autobiography System (Model GE-TW-2000A) is reusable, so you can enjoy it again and again.

CAUTION: PROLONGED USE MAY CAUSE DROWSINESS.

42

"The Secret Language of Custom"

Evelyn H.

*Evelyn, a high school student, explains how she has
come to understand and appreciate the food, culture,
and language of her Ukrainian heritage.*

I am a foreigner in my grandparents' house. I roam, mapless,
through a land whose cabbage smells and babushka dolls amaze
and terrify me. Even the light shines differently there, with the not-
quite-rightness of light on unfamiliar territory: it's at a different
angle and one shade shy of normal. Without a compass, I navigate
the choppy seas of an unknown language, drowning with each sing-
songy wave. Just as I'm about to go under a life preserver, English,
is thrown at my head.

"Ev-lon," my grandma pleads. "Come on, have some more to
eat. You don't even have any mashed potatoes! Shame on you!" She
slaps a spoonful of snow-white, too-salty potatoes on my plate—her
idea of love, my idea of punishment.

My family spends every major holiday with my Ukrainian grandparents, and with each gravy-laden meal, I've felt more and more like
a tourist in a foreign land. There was a time when my grandparents
did not confuse me nearly as much. When I was young, I thought
everyone's grandparents were "Baba" and "Didi" and thought nothing
of eating Ukrainian food on Christmas Eve; surely every family ate
pyrohy (potato or sauerkraut-filled dumplings), holubtsi (barley-filled

cabbage rolls) and mashed potatoes with dill gravy. I never questioned the Easter tradition of waiting with my grandpa at the Ukrainian church for our basket to be blessed. Standing in that stale church, looking up at all the round, wrinkled faces, I felt strangely protected. I liked the predictability of custom. Each year, I was delighted anew when the priest came by with his blessed-water splashing apparatus: a pint-sized, ornate bucket in which he dipped an aspergill. I anticipated the moment when he would approach us and, with a flick of his wrist, send a holy shower raining down upon our basket of kielbasa, cheese, hard-boiled eggs, salt and pepper, babka bread and a cross carved in butter. "Kristos vos cress," my grandpa's voice would boom. "Christ has risen." Eye-level with the basket, I would watch, mesmerized, as the water droplets danced across the melting butter's surface.

It wasn't until later that I cast a suspicious eye on my grandparents and their customs. I distinctly remember the first time I refused my grandma's gravy—an eleven-year-old's act of rebellion. My mother, father, brother, uncle, grandma, grandpa and I were seated at my grandparents' table, my grandpa at the head, my brother and I opposite him. My grandma sat nearest the kitchen. After a Thanksgiving prayer, said first in English by my father and echoed in Ukrainian by my grandpa, the food was passed. I reluctantly plopped a bit of everything on my plate, but when the warm gravy boat landed in my hands, I passed it to my brother. I knew exactly what I was doing. When I was five, I'd delighted my grandma by exclaiming, "I want too much gravy!" At eleven, I was done being her Too-Much-Gravy Girl.

My father noticed what I'd done first. "Have some gravy!" he mouthed. I pretended not to understand. "Evelyn, have some gravy!" he unintentionally said aloud. My mother and grandparents halted their animated Ukrainian conversation. Uncle Mark threw me a glance that said, "You don't realize what you've done." I sat there, pretending to be confused. "What?" I questioned their incredulity.

"Ev-lon," my grandma began. "I made that gravy just for you," she lied. I could see I'd hurt her feelings. "You have to eat some." Everyone stared.

"Evelyn, just eat some gravy," my mother said, exasperated.

"Ev-lon, what is wrong with you? You always loved my gravy!" My grandma got up and walked away from the table.

"Fine, okay, I'll have some," I said. I'd had no idea gravy meant so much to my grandma.

I am just now beginning to learn the secret language of my grandparents' customs. We have to eat babka bread on Easter because my great-grandpa, a baker, baked it for days before Easter. My grandma misses the smell that filled the bakery; she misses helping him stir the raisins into the dough and the way the bakery would slowly fill to capacity with dome-shaped breads. To her, Easter is babka bread. I've also learned that we have to eat our Christmas Eve dinner at night because in Ukraine, the festivities can begin only after the first star is seen.

I've made headway in this land of sauerkraut. The proof came last Christmas when the infamous gravy boat again landed in my hands. I looked at its contents, the noxious dill odor steaming back at me. I looked at my grandma; she was watching me. Uh oh, I thought. Do I take the gravy and assimilate, or stand my ground? My grandma answered for me. "You don't have to eat it if you don't want to. You're still my Too-Much-Gravy Girl, though."

With that, my visa was extended for another year.

43

"Language Heads Down the Rabbit Hole"

John Schwartz

Schwartz bemoans the rapidity with which new words and phrases are tumbling out of the business world into our everyday lives. While granting that language is continuously evolving, he would prefer that we be more discerning in our word choices in order to avoid confusing and slippery meanings.

In Times Square the other morning, I noticed that the news display on the tower at 1 Times Square, the famous "Zipper," was not working.

"The Zipper's down," I said to myself, and smiled at the unintended pun. It's only one example of the ways that the words used to describe the technologies that suffuse society have composed a second language—an argot that sounds like everyday English, but which has different meanings.

Words like "Zipper" and "down" are not jargon—incomprehensible words used to describe things that may or may not be incomprehensible, but which give the speaker the cachet of incomprehensibility. (Saying your machine has had a "General Protection Fault" sounds much more important than simply saying it's "all messed up.") Nor are they, strictly speaking, slang, which consists of newly minted words like "phat" or "wack" or, once upon a time, "groovy" or "hep." Instead, technospeak involves layering new meanings over familiar words.

Language, of course, is continually evolving. And using common words in uncommon contexts isn't reserved for technology or business. Physicists give the properties of subatomic particles strange and charming modifiers like "strange" and "charm." But new coinages are accelerating in these go-go, wired (and now, wireless) days.

"Technology is arguably the most fruitful source of new words in English, and a lot of technology words come through business," said Wendalyn Nichols, editorial director of the reference division at Random House. As many as 300 terms enter the Random House Webster's College Dictionary each year, of which some 200 might come from technology, she says. Among recent additions are the irksome "e-tailing" and the clever "clicks and mortar," which aptly describes traditional retailers (with brick-and-mortar stores) that expand into the mouse-click world of the Internet.

The way business tries to spin new meanings out of old words often grates on the ear and the mind. Listen as the highly paid pitchman gushes that his company offers the leading product in a particular "space," or that his Web site is getting more "eyeballs" than the competition, or that his site, because it holds those eyeballs a little longer than its rivals, is "sticky." It's not enough to engineer an advertising campaign that relies on word-of-mouth referral by consumers: these days, the au courant agency calls it "viral marketing."

These buzzwords, strung together, lose even the little meaning they started with. How can the tech types talk about making their Web "portals" "sticky"? Doors are something to go *through*—you only linger there during an earthquake.

"Repurposing" common words as slang irritates Gareth Branwyn, who writes the Jargon Watch column for Wired magazine. His writing celebrates the wit underlying such geeky neologisms as saying someone is "404" when a knock on the door goes unanswered—a sly re-use of the message "404 not found," which Web surfers encounter whenever they try to log on to a site that has vanished into the ether.

Mr. Branwyn's gripe with the way conventional words are made slang is twofold. First, he says, "There's no humor in it." Second, while all slang helps its initiates feel superior to outsiders, "there's an inherent dishonesty" in turning common words into slang, he says, because it attempts to make the people uncomfortable on their own turf, as if they were outsiders.

This forced march toward new meanings can create costly inefficiencies, says Michael Schrage, co-director of the E-markets initiative at the Media Laboratory of the Massachusetts Institute of Technology. "When the same word means different things to different people, you're going to spend more time managing meaning than managing the problem," he warned.

What words mean and how slippery those meanings can be was a subject to which Ludwig Wittgenstein, one of the century's most celebrated and difficult philosophers, devoted much of his waking life. The playwright Tom Stoppard, who studied Wittgenstein, put the protean potential of words hilariously to work in the play "Dogg's Hamlet, Cahout's Macbeth." Mr. Stoppard imagined a new language, "Dogg," in which "plank" means "ready," "block" means "next," "slab" means "O.K." and "cube" means "thank you." Dogg is being spoken onstage by several schoolboys, when a newcomer shows up who speaks plain English.

The newcomer, whose name is Easy, assumes he understands the conversation until, asking for a plank, he is handed a cube. The misunderstandings escalate: when the school headmaster calls Easy a "moronic creep," he is understandably offended, not understanding that the headmaster is actually talking about his carpet. But what can you expect when the phrase in Dogg for "Do you have the time, sir?" is "Cretinous pig-faced git"?

Now we all live in Mr. Stoppard's world. Or, just maybe, it's the world imagined by that original semiotician egghead, Humpty Dumpty.

"There's glory for you!" Mr. Dumpty proclaimed to a mystified Alice, in "Through the Looking Glass."

Alice, playing the role we all play when confronted with linguistic nonsense, responds, "I don't know what you mean by glory."

> Humpty Dumpty smiled contemptuously. "Of course you don't—till I tell you. I meant 'there's a nice knock-down argument for you!'"
>
> "But 'glory' doesn't mean 'a nice knock-down argument,'" Alice objected.
>
> "When I use a word," Humpty Dumpty said in a rather a scornful tone, "it means just what I choose it to mean—neither more nor less."
>
> "The question is," said Alice, "whether you can make words mean different things."
>
> "The question is," said Humpty Dumpty, "which is to be master—that's all."

Today there are dot-com Humpty Dumptys all over the place, making words mean what they want them to mean, just as they've attempted to redefine stock valuations and the whole meaning of the term "business plan." Many of them are now failing. That might have little to do with the way they have mangled the language. But then again, it may.

Words, elastic and versatile though they may be, still have to mean something. And treating them as if they can be shaped whichever way we like instead of seeing them as the solid planks from which reality is built isn't so different from assuming that businesses don't have to make a profit, or that stock prices will rise forever.

It is, in other words, just the kind of pride that goeth before a Great Fall. The whole situation leaves me feeling a bit mimsy.

44

"Cinematic Grammar," from *Reading the Movies: Twelve Great Films on Video and How to Teach Them*

William V. Costanzo

"The key to understanding any grammar is to understand the language as a system." Costanzo goes on to explain the hidden language codes of film so that we may have a better understanding of how to read and comprehend film.

The key to understanding any grammar is to understand the language as a system. Think of film as a system of images and sounds. The images may represent real objects, imaginary events, even ideas. The sounds may include music, sound effects, or speech. Filmmakers arrange these images and sounds systematically. The arrangement is meaningful to us because we understand the system. Let's take a short film sequence as an example. First, we see the image of a man standing on a bridge, a rope around his neck. Next, we see a close-up of his face. Beads of sweat form on his forehead. As he shuts his eyes, we hear the first strains of some banjo music. Then we see the image of a woman, elegantly dressed and smiling, seated on a garden swing and swaying gently to the music. Her motion is exceptionally slow. What does this sequence mean? How do we interpret it? We may guess that the man is about to be hanged. The rope and sweat are clues to his predicament. But what do the music and the woman have to do with him? Maybe there is someone on the bridge with a banjo. Maybe this woman is watching the event. More likely, though, the music and the woman represent his thoughts. We know that slow motion and special music in a movie often signal a flashback, a quick visit to the past. The fact that this slow-motion image follows a close-up of the man's face suggests that his mind is focused on the past. So we read the sequence as a subjective event: The man is thinking of his loved one at the moment of his death. What enables us to make sense of a film like this is our understanding of the systems of images and sounds, close-ups, and flashbacks through which filmmakers communicate meaning.

Photography can be regarded as a signifying system because photographs, like words, refer to things beyond themselves. A snapshot of a cat is not a cat, or else we couldn't slip it into our wallet. Yet photographs are more like the things they represent than words are. Photographs are likenesses; they bear a visual resemblance to some material original. Words usually are arbitrary sounds; the sounds represented by the letters c-a-t have no obvious similarity to the animal. That's why a non-native speaker is more likely to understand the picture than the word.

Those who study signifying systems—semioticians or semiologists, as they are sometimes called—make a crucial distinction between a signifier and what it signifies. The sound and image of the word *cat* (its pronunciation and its spelling on the page) are *signifiers*. What speakers think of when using the word *cat* is the *signified*. The signified is not the animal itself, but a conception. Most likely that conception involves mental images and personal associations formed through years of contact with furry, feline creatures. Semioticians use the term *sign* for the relationship between a signifier and the signified. A verbal sign is the relation between a sound-image and a concept. The actual animal—the thing to which the sign refers—its *referent*—is something else again. We'll leave that part to the zoologists.

What then is a photographic sign? Like a verbal sign, a photographic sign is a relation between the signifier and the signified. In this case, the signifier is the photographic image—patterns of shade and color on the screen—and the signified is the mental image—what those patterns evoke in our imagination. Because motion pictures are so lifelike, it's easy to forget that the signifier (what is projected on the screen) is not the signified (what we project in our imagination), or that the sign (a relation between the perceptual image and our conceptual response to it) is not the referent (what was in front of the lens when the camera was turned on). It's as if images of the world are transferred directly to the film stock, to the movie screen, and then to the inner screens of people in the audience, with very little effort or translation. This may help to explain why movies seem so real and why we rarely give much credit to the viewers for the mental work involved.

Yet it is important to remember that watching movies is an interpretative act. Despite the remarkable realism of photography, a photograph is still a sign, and signs must be read. Some images are more abstract than others. When Picasso represents a cat with a few circles and some squiggly lines, his drawing may be more challenging to read than, say, a painting by Mary Cassatt, especially by someone unfamiliar with the ways of abstract art. Similarly, Cassatt's painting or a Japanese woodblock print may be harder to read than a modern documentary film on cars. We can imagine a spectrum of signs ranging from the most abstract to the most specific. Words are more abstract than images, and drawings generally are more abstract than photographs. While the word *car* may represent any year or make of automobile, a pencil sketch begins to look more like a sports car or a sedan, and a photograph is more specific still.

The specificity of film creates special problems in interpretation. Writers can use words like *vehicle, automobile, station wagon,* or *Volvo* to indicate different levels of abstraction, but how do we know the intention of a filmmaker when what we see on the screen are 1985 Jaguars or 1990 Coupes de Ville? It seems that the language of speech is better equipped than the language of pictures for making direct statements. When I say, "This car is old," or "that car is fast,"

I'm making an assertion. But when I film a certain car, I'm not so sure how it will appear to viewers. I may manipulate the image to emphasize the car's age or speed, but essentially the image is a presentation rather than a statement. In this sense, visual and verbal texts require complementary forms of interpretation. Images evoke assertions; words evoke images. The audience completes the message by supplying mental words or pictures.

45

"Hip-Hop Becoming a Worldwide Language for Youth Resistance"

The selection describes the culture, music, and language of the world of hip-hop and how it has influenced youth around the world.

Many middle-class parents thought it was just a fad when their adolescents and teenagers started wearing baggy jeans that sagged below their hips in imitation of hip-hop culture. However, it did not pass. Almost 30 years after hip-hop got its start in the black urban scene of the 1970s, this complex, riveting mixture of sound, rhythm, dress, attitude, and poetics has become a universal, underground culture for youth resistance around the globe, maintains Halifu Osumare, a faculty member at the University of Hawaii, Honolulu.

In 1999, rap—one of four components of hip-hop culture—became the top-selling music genre in America. "It began in black and Latino American communities, but you can't go to any youth culture in any capital city on the globe today where you won't find rappers talking about their marginalization using similar lyrics, similar music, and similar dress," Osumare points out. She has found, in research on hip-hop cultures in Japan, England, France, and Germany, that youths in each region adapt American patterns to their own demographics:

- In London, marginalized East Indian youth blend Indian melodies and Hindi with English rap as a street form of protest.

- In Paris, poor Jewish, Middle Eastern, and West African youth coming out of the projects use hip-hop styles and rap to talk about their poverty and police brutality, as exemplified in a French video called "La Haine" ("Hate").

- In Japan, female hip-hoppers use the genre to defy gender restrictions for women.

"Hip-hop has become a universal tool for talking back to the mainstream of any society," Osumare notes. However, the very success of this genre has created something of a schism in hip-hop culture, according to Osumare and Michael Barnes, a graduate student in sociology at the University of California, Berkeley, who is also a disc jockey and was one of her teaching assistants when she taught a course on "Power Moves: Hip-Hop Culture and Sociology" at Berkeley.

Community-based underground rappers are drowned out by the mass appeal and commercialization of the big-time, best-selling artists, some of whom are marketing a gangster persona with songs that focus on health, possessions, and crime, often with a misogynistic attitude toward women, Barnes argues. Although the "gangsta" style arose in New York, Philadelphia, and Los Angeles in the early 1990s as an authentic expression of the grinding poverty, mass unemployment, and prison experience of ghetto youth, he believes it has been appropriated in recent years by "studio playas," who don't come from that background and are in it only for the money.

These guys are ultra capitalists who glorify materialism. Whether these playas are as rich as they say they are is up for debate, but they definitely appeal to the outlaw, antiestablishment tendencies of American culture, and the music industry capitalizes on that. You can't tell in the beginning if a studio playa comes from poverty, as he claims, but if he becomes famous, he can't hide it, and authenticity matters. It certainly does. Now you hear songs not just criticizing the establishment, but calling [other rappers] out, saying, "This isn't right for hip-hop culture. Fine. You're making money, but what are you going to do for the community?"

"Hip-hop is incredibly diverse," Barnes maintains. "More underground artists are doing substantive, in-depth social criticism, and you're starting to see more youth-based movements based on hip-hop." He says the activism of hip-hop culture shows itself when a large number of artists come together to put out an entire album on specific issues, such as the "Hip-Hop for Respect" album, done in reaction to the Amadou Diallo shooting in New York; "Mumia 911," dedicated to Mumia Abu-Jamal, who is on death row in Pennsylvania for killing a police officer; or "America Is Dying Slowly," an album on the ravages of AIDS in the black community. Only by listening to their music do outsiders know what is going on with urban youth, whether black, Asian, Latino, or of any other ethnicity, Barnes insists.

46

"Double-Talk"

Rick Bass

*The clinical language of industry is slowly replacing
the words we use to talk about wilderness. Words
are more than superficial language. They are store-
houses of interpretation that depend on the cultural
setting of their birth and the political and social
intentions of the creator. Bass asks, "What are the
consequences of a language that does not properly
respect its subject?"*

Next to vision, I believe language is our strongest sense. Allow
me, then, some time to lament the corporate manipulation of
my craft. To one who loves both language and wild country, it's infu-
riating to see the two loves pitted against each other, language being
used to suck out the last good and vital marrow of wild country.

It's a platitude that big business runs the country, and frankly,
whenever writers do battle with the monied interests, we expect to
lose more than we win. But we writers like to think that at least we
can help shape the future, by creating a purer, more mythical world
in which the right thing is done, the right decision is made, and dignity, beauty, and nobility abound.

We can't. If anything, we're losing these battles even more deci-
sively than we're losing the money wars.

Just as the forests, the wild prairies, the ocean, and the deserts are being taken from us, so, too—like an echo, or perhaps a fore-shadowing—the language of wild places is being taken from us, insidiously, slyly, steadily. We are being given instead the language of machines, the language of the sick and the diseased. Individual words, used daily in government agencies, cede vast amounts of wild territory every time they are uttered. These words obscure the true beauty of wilderness and the possibility that there might exist a few landscapes that can do just fine without the curse of all our help and knowledge.

Clearcuts, for instance, are no longer exclusively called clearcuts. The straightforward old Anglo-Saxon word has been replaced in most cases with the sinuous, almost lisping *seed trees with reserves,* which sounds more like some sort of Individual Retirement Account than a forest. Clearcuts are surrounded by "shelterbelts"—little more than beauty strips designed to obscure the public's view of the car-nage beyond.

Engineers speak of the road "prism" as they make plans to enter the last roadless cores in benign fashion—the word *prism* conjuring not only the stability of the Pyramids but also, more subtly, the friendly kaleidoscopes of one's childhood. Where are the slaughterous runoffs of spring beneath that word *prism*? Where are the slumpage and col-lapse of roads, the sedimentation of streams, the crushing fragmen-tation of habitat?

Prescribed treatment. This phrase is used to describe an activity proposed by the Forest Service or some other agency—and rest as-sured, it usually involves chainsaws. Implicit in this notion of a pre-scription is that nature is sick, and we are the physician. That is not to say that there are not places where natural processes ("historic vegetative patterns") have not become slightly, temporarily unbal-anced as a result of our past mistakes and transgressions, nor do I think that there aren't places where we can "manipulate" the for-est to bring it closer to what most of us might describe as "health." But we use the terms *prescription* and *treatment* for every timber sale in the national forests. If your goal is to help preserve the sanctity, mystery, awe, and power of wild places, the battle is already half lost every time you open your mouth.

What are the cumulative effects of such usage—this daily refashioning of the woods into a thing that not only can but should always be controlled and manipulated?

How much room remains in that kind of language for what we are running out of, which is wilderness?

As a longtime resident of a logging community, and as a weekly respondent to one proposed logging project after another, I am every bit as guilty of using this language. Not only do I use it in my letters of entreaty and outrage, I find myself sometimes *thinking* in that other language as I walk through the woods. Instead of seeing a fallen, rotting nurse log that feeds insects and nurtures plants and soil, I see diseased trees, pathogens, fiber "wasted," value that is not "captured" in timely fashion.

Instead of seeing the mysteries of mycelium, I see root rot and dwarf mistletoe, and my mind skips ahead to the obvious "application": Fell the fir, girdle the larch. Stop the progress of death and dying. Stop the creation of new soil.

When a lot of trees in the wilderness die for one reason or another, then fall down or blow over, why is it called "fuel loading," rather than, say, "a bounty of carbon"? How did we lose even this battle? Is it the forests that elicit from us this exceptional deviousness of language? At first I think it is, but grassland activist George Wuerthner tells me about similar abuses of language in the prairies and the desert. "When the Bureau of Land Management is spending taxpayer money to develop water sources on public wildlands to benefit cow owners," he says, "they call them 'range-improvement' funds. But the only thing being improved is the ability to raise cows."

Wuerthner continues, "They call grazing a 'tool,' as a way of justifying livestock use of the land. There is 'Wildlife Services,' which serves wildlife by killing it. There is the 'Conservation

Fund,' which pays for the eradication of prairie dogs with federal dollars."

In the depths of the sea, the language of wild and natural ecosystems is also egregiously abused. Carl Safina, author of *Song for the Blue Ocean* (and an Audubon Society vice-president), points out, "Fisheries people talk incessantly of 'harvesting' fishes, and even of 'harvesting' whales—trying to impart an agricultural tone, as though firing a bomb into the body of the largest creature ever to live on earth is analogous to picking watermelons that have been planted and cultivated."

Wuerthner agrees: "We see it with regard to hunting, where hunters don't kill wildlife, they 'harvest' it. Well, I don't harvest deer or elk, I kill them, and I'm quite willing to accept the proper term instead of hiding in some farm terminology."

This damning notion that natural resources are endless, controllable, easily manipulated to our desires is aided and abetted by the inability of wildlife to stand still and be quantified. Safina laments the use of the word *stock*—as if fish are but shoes on a shelf—and the glib interchangeability of two words, *fish* and *fishery*, that should not be interchangeable at all.

"In a trout stream," he says, "the trout themselves are not the fishery. They are simply fish—a population of wild animals. The people standing in the water in rubber pants are the fishery. On the Grand Banks, the weary cod and halibut are the fish; the boats whose wakes crisscross overhead as they pull the nets are the fishery."

The list of language abuses seems endless. In the forest, cyclic peaks of insect activity—exerting a healthy, selective force upon the living grace of the forest, providing nurse logs and hollow snags, recycling nutrients—are now called "outbreaks." In reality the insects are more surgeons than we will ever be, one of the forces that have shaped and carved the wild landscapes into their mosaic of health, much as wolves have whittled, in the words of the poet Robinson Jeffers, "the fleet limbs of the antelope."

Catastrophic fires? We use these terms freely in our dialogue with the government agencies, but would we ever have the temerity to suggest that postindustrial management of the public lands has been its own kind of "catastrophic" event? Why is industry so comfortable using such terms of extremity, even violence? Such is the continuing, daily diminishment of wilderness in this country.

Who defines for us what language to use and not use, when we may and may not speak? In a true democracy, in true freedom, would we be making these choices for ourselves? Would we recognize when language comes from the heart, versus when it is just trying to sell a product?

I fear increasingly that even as the wild country around us is being compromised, like beach sand crumbling at the touch of the waves, so, too, is our language of wilderness crumbling beneath us, until one day our country will have forgotten how even to talk about wilderness, or grizzly bears, or any of the other vanishing things, and the shadows, the stories they cast.

I have been pleading on behalf of the last roadless cores in Montana and the Yaak Valley for so long now that I rarely use the word *tree* anymore. Instead I choose the more familiar *timber*, whether the trees are still standing or not. Dead and dying trees are usually called "material." Even the relatively benign phrase *woody debris* sounds like something you might comb out of your dog's hair after a hard day hunting: an annoyance, a nuisance. Often when there are a lot of dead, mulchy, crumbling logs in a stand (delicate fairy slipper orchids growing out of that soft duff and powder, a richness of mushrooms), the official agency language will speak of how the groves need "sanitation."

How funny. It's in these tangled, unsanitary places that I like to sit and rest, mesmerized by the intricacy of deadfall and blowdown, secure in the faith that in such a forest, even in what looks to me like unstructured chaos, there is grace and order and design. I cannot name it or prove it or even see it, but sitting there in its midst, I can feel it, all around me.

"When sea turtles that have drowned in nets wash up on beaches, they are often referred to as 'stranded,'" says Safina. "I have been in meetings with fishery managers who did not understand that all the 'stranded' turtles the fishermen were dismissing as 'not a problem' were, in fact, dead. These are washed-up turtle carcasses, not stranded turtles."

Regeneration harvest? The forest is whacked and stacked, exposed to the brutal, drying heat of an unprotected moonscape; and then little drifting-in seedlings are expected to "regenerate." You "harvest" by taking it all. I think I'll just keep using the word *clearcut*.

What are the consequences of a language that does not properly respect its subject?

This is certainly nothing that scientists can analyze, and yet I believe it is as real and significant a cumulative stress upon the ultimate future of the wilderness, and its wild inhabitants, as exists. Let the last few wild places escape the curse of our language and retain their eloquence. Let's keep the last precious bit as it is, rotting and burning and regenerating at its own pace and rhythm: a place where bears can be most fully bears, and where poets can be most fully poets, and even, perhaps, where scientists can be most fully scientists. Our dwindling wilderness areas should remain the greatest living sanctuaries on earth for our long, long list of endangered and threatened and sensitive species. But they are also one of the greatest available textbooks on the true possibilities of language, story, character, and imagination—both in individuals and in communities. We need to protect and preserve the last dark forest gardens, the last few unprotected public wildlands. But please, let's not go in there and "ecosystem manage" them.

Sometimes it seems as if our language is becoming as fragmented and manipulated as the dwindling wild landscape itself. I want more, not less, of the kind of landscape that reminds us that the wonders of life can exceed even the finest reaches of our language. We have enough, more than enough, of the chained and roaded, paved-over and cut-over lands, so subservient to our short-term hungers. We can never re-create our last few wildlands after they are gone or altered. We can only protect them, and treasure them—or, if we fail, tell stories about them after they are gone, with the echo of language.

47

"Technicality," from *Science and Language Links: Classroom Implications*

Beverly Derewianka

*If high school students are to understand science texts,
they need to know how the people who write the texts
organize the concepts to be learned. Science, like all
other disciplines, has a language of its own that
prescribes a certain way of looking at the world.
This selection provides an introduction to the basic
organization of the language of science.*

Each subject area explores how the world works in its own distinctive way. These different ways of construing the world are reflected in the language of the discipline. At the most basic level this can be seen in the specialist terminology that has evolved to meet the needs of each of these areas. Many regard this terminology as unnecessary jargon that simply confuses students. It is important, however, to realize the function of technical terms. They are used by scientists to refer to aspects of their field in ways that are unambiguous and convey exactly the same meaning to anyone else working in the field. This is crucial in a discipline that depends so much on such notions as reliability, precision and replicability. Attaching commonly understood labels to shared understandings is also an efficient way of operating. It means that the technical term can be used as a form of shorthand between colleagues, avoiding the necessity of having to constantly explain a concept or process.

If we are serious about inducting students into the discipline of science, then they need to be comfortable with the language of science. They need access to this language (and to the concepts behind the language) in order to participate in the discourse of science. A science textbook cannot therefore avoid the use of technical terms. The dilemma for textbook writers and teachers is how to introduce this terminology without alienating the students. Most well-written junior science textbooks would approach a topic from an everyday perspective, helping the students to identify with the ideas involved. The concept in question would be developed in familiar language as much as possible, perhaps accompanied by hands-on activities and oral exploration. The students would then be moved on to the less "commonsense" notions and into the more "scientific" ways of conceiving of the world. At this point the scientific terminology comes into play. When a term is first introduced, it is printed in bold letters to indicate that a definition can be found at this point. To consolidate the understanding, a number of examples are often given. For example:

> *Compounds* are pure substances which can be split up by chemical means. This is because compounds are made of two or more elements chemically joined together. *Water* contains hydrogen and oxygen. *Carbon dioxide* contains carbon and oxygen. *Sugar* contains the elements carbon, hydrogen and oxygen chemically joined together. *The World of Science*, p. 57

Introduced in this way, technical terms need not be seen as a source of difficulty in reading a scientific text. In fact for students of non-English-speaking background in particular, the technical terminology presents fewer problems than everyday words with less precisely defined meanings.

In addition to the technicality encountered in science textbooks, the level of abstraction in these texts is likely to cause problems in reading for many students. Much scientific knowledge is of an abstract nature—and this is increasingly the case as students move through secondary school.

One grammatical resource characteristic of scientific abstraction is nominalization. This refers to the common practice in science of changing a "process" into a "thing" (or an abstraction). In the chapter on Elements, for example, the properties of metals are expressed in more process terms using verbs:

1. How well can the metal conduct electricity?
2. How well can the metal conduct heat?
3. How easily can the metal be hammered or flattened into sheets?
4. How easily can the metal be drawn into wires?
5. Does the metal break when you try to bend it?
6. Does the surface of the metal look dull, glassy or metallic?
7. What are the metal's melting and boiling points?

In scientific text, these processes are generally turned into abstract "things" (or nouns), such as conductivity, malleability, ductility, and so on.

This has the effect of summing up the process and enabling the text to move on. Having described the process of how a metal and the gases in the air react together, we can from then on refer to this process using the noun, "corrosion." This can be illustrated in an excerpt from Chapter 4, Elements, in *The World of Science*.

The chemical activity of a metal helps determine how it is separated from its ore. There are two main methods:

1. The less active metals are extracted in a blast furnace, for example, iron, lead.

2. The more active metals are extracted using
   electricity, for example, aluminum, sodium.

We can do both of these extractions in the laboratory.

The processes ("extracted") have now become a thing ("extractions").

Once a process has become a "thing," it is able to enter into relationships with other things. This facilitates the scientific endeavor of trying to identify relationships within the world. A scientist is able, for example, to describe the relative degrees of malleability, reactivity, resistance and conductivity of one metal as opposed to another, without going into longwinded explanations each time of the various properties.

Even at the junior secondary level, textbooks abound with nominalizations. In the chapter from *The World of Science* on Elements, for example, we constantly come across nominalizations such as the following:

- The activity series

- Good conductors of heat

- Its ease of extraction

- Chemical reactions

- Natural sources

- These extractions

- The rate of corrosion

Compared with a senior secondary science text, however, the junior texts are extremely considerate of their readers. The abstraction and compactness of senior texts makes huge demands on the reader. In just two years, the readers of our sample text will be faced with the following in their senior text:

The **measured conductivity** of very pure forms of the carbon allotropes graphite and diamond indicate that carbon is the best **thermal conductor** of all the elements. The **conductivity** of these solids is very sensitive to **impurities** and trace amounts can cause marked **reduction** in **conductivity**. Wiecek, C. *Chemistry for Senior Students*, p. 19

In oral language, we tend to "unpack" the nominalizations (in bold) by changing them back into their verbal form. For example, we might have said something like:

If we take very pure forms of graphite and diamond, which are carbon allotropes, and measure how well they conduct heat, we would find that carbon is able to conduct heat the best of all the elements. These solids are very sensitive to impurities. Even a tiny amount of an impurity can greatly reduce how well they are able to conduct heat.

Students who have not been exposed to nominalizations through sustained reading of scientific texts will most likely find the highly nominalized prose of senior textbooks quite daunting. While some authors overuse nominalization when they could have written in a more reader-friendly way, it is nevertheless an integral and functional part of scientific prose and cannot be completely avoided. Students need to become accustomed to both reading nominalized text and using nominalizations in their own writing. Teachers aware of this potential difficulty (and some uses of nominalization are more likely to cause trouble than others) can draw the students' attention to such forms as they read and can "unpack" the nominalizations if necessary (or ask the students to unpack them, perhaps by retelling the sentence or text in the way they would say it orally).

48

"Comic Books," from A Book of Puzzlements: Play and Invention with Language

Herbert Kohl

Comic books are filled with intricate and subtle designs and content. Young people are often more knowledgeable than adults about how they work. Kohl introduces the forms for expressing language in the world of comic books, one of the most versatile formats for presenting complex language and thought in a short and seemingly simple way.

Comics are not simple structurally. Basically they consist of rectangles that contain characters with bubbles coming from their mouths. But this description is deceptively simple. There are many types of bubbles: the forms of comic book art are quite sophisticated and they make it possible for thoughts, dreams, narrative, and dialogue to be expressed in a single frame. There are smooth bubbles that end in arrows. These represent talk, the arrow pointing to the talker. There are also compound bubbles (called more talk) which make it possible for a single character to say several different things in one frame.

For example, if someone is shot, it is possible by connecting three smooth bubbles to have one character say "There's trouble," "Watch out, you," and "Are you hurt?" all in one box on a page. The joined bubbles represent past, present, and future, whereas the picture has to show one moment. In this case the picture can show a menacing figure, a shot fired, or a body. Although the picture has one temporal dimension the bubbles expand the scene to cover several minutes.

There are dream and thought bubbles too. These are more undulating. There are lots of curves in the bubble, and instead of an arrow going to the speaker, a series of bubbles goes to the speaker indicating that the words are thought but not spoken.

Interesting combinations are possible. It is possible to represent thoughts and words at the same time. For example, if a person hates another but has to seem nice, the dialogue can be represented by this combination of bubbles:

There are three more common comic book forms. One is the spiked bubble that indicates a shout or a denial or a protest. It is like an exclamation point, and usually spiked bubbles are used sparsely to indicate pain, struggle, or serious intent. The other form is the long rectangular shape that appears in almost every frame in comics. It is written by the narrator of the story and carries the movement along from one point to another. There are many different kinds of narrative voices that appear in comic books. Sometimes one of the characters in the story is telling about what happens and the voice is "I." There are other comic books in which the illustrator talks directly to the reader, makes jokes, and comments on the story (as in *Spider Man*). In some comics the narrator is omniscient like the narrator of many novels. He or she can see or know what's happening in many different places and at many different times and has more knowledge of every situation than any of the characters. It's fun to read a batch of comics solely to figure out how they use the narrative voice.

> ONE DAY I FOUND
> A NOTE ON MY DESK. . .

> HERE'S SOOPER DOOPER
> AGAIN. . .HE'S TIRED.

> AT THAT MOMENT--ON
> PLANET X, A MAN WOKE

The third form is what could be called the "zap" word. Zap words are words that indicate sounds or actions, and are drawn to look like what they represent. They aren't spoken by the characters and are part of the atmosphere of the world of comics. Here are a few common zaps:

Putting these forms together, you can easily represent a complex action in a single panel:

The following is a comic strip without characters. Try to give it content—and to develop comics of your own using all the forms described here.

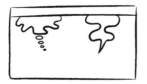

In addition to the comic book forms there are some themes that are common. One of the most popular ones has to do with the origins of superheroes. Concern with origins isn't confined to comic book characters, of course. "Where did I come from and how did I get to be the way I am?" are questions we all ask sometime in our lives. These questions seem to be as old as language. Every mythology begins with accounts of origins—how the earth came to be, why there is order instead of chaos, how people were created, why people walk upright, how language was made, how food and shelter originated. Here, for example, is an Eskimo origin tale:

> There was once a girl who lived in the open desert of white snow. One day she went in a boat with a man who suddenly threw her into the sea. When she tried to hold on to the side of the boat he cut her fingers off so that the boat would not turn over. She sank to the bottom of the sea where she made her home inside a large bubble. Here she became the mother of all life in the sea. The fingers she had lost grew into seals and walruses. And the people of this frozen land now had food to eat. Now they had skins for warmth. Now they had oil for the long nights of winter.

This tale is not as arbitrary as it might seem. The mother of all life in the sea is a person who has been harmed. She lost her fingers, yet they became food for people. What we are and what we eat are not that dissimilar. There is a unity to life that must be respected. The destructive can become creative but we must respect this relation-ship because those that suffer death nurture us. This simple story embodies a way of looking at people and their relationship to nature.

Comic book superheroes are mythical figures created in our time. The stories of their origins reveal aspects of our culture just as the Eskimo myth displayed some values of that culture. Take Superman, for example. He is an alien, born on the planet Krypton, which was destroyed in an atomic holocaust. He was saved by his parents, sent to earth where he is stronger and purer than the rest of us. The alien Superman becomes our hero and savior. He is not one of us and only presents a human appearance through Clark Kent, his earthly identity. In order to exist on an everyday level he has to disguise himself as one of us.

Wonder Woman is similar. She was born on Paradise Island where no men lived. Her mother was Queen Hippolyte and her original name was Princess Diana. During the Second World War an American pilot, Steve Trevor, crashed on Paradise Island and Princess Diana fell in love with him. Eventually, she had to choose between love of him and loyalty to the Amazons on Paradise Island. One of the early Wonder Woman comics discussed her choice:

> And so Princess Diana, the Wonder Woman, giving up her heritage, and her right to eternal life, leaves Paradise Island to take the man she loves back to America—the land she learns to love and protect, and adopts as her own!

Again, an alien comes to rescue us. This time her motive is love. For Superman the motive was to prevent the earth from destroying itself the way Krypton did.

The Hulk is a more recent superhero, and the story of his origin reverses that of Superman and Wonder Woman. He was born a hu-man, Bruce Banner, who became a famous nuclear physicist. In ex-perimenting with physical forces beyond his control, Dr. Banner found himself transformed into the Hulk—a superhuman although subintelligent force. Bruce Banner and the Hulk are a contemporary version of Dr. Jekyll and Mr. Hyde. It is never clear however whether the Hulk is a positive or a negative force. When science gets the upper hand is it a positive or negative force? That is the problem posed by the Hulk.

The Hulk reminds me of the Golem, a figure in Yiddish mythology. The Golem is compressed out of the letters of the Hebrew alphabet and is a giant force similar to the Hulk. The Golem has an aleph (the first letter of the Hebrew alphabet) imprinted on its head. When the Golem is called forth (by a rabbi or mystic who can unleash the power of the alphabet) it can be used to destroy evil. However, once it gets its job done it keeps on destroying what is around it until someone erases the aleph from its head. As a force the Golem can be used for good purposes, but it is itself neither good nor evil. Like most force its effectiveness depends on how it is controlled.

Mythology is open-ended. We can all create our own villains and superheroes. One way to involve young people in writing and in making comic books is to ask them to create their own superheroes. Usually first efforts will imitate what is already in the comics or on TV. That is where origins can help people develop and clarify their own creations. After making up a superhero, it makes sense to create adventures.

However, writing, creating comic books, or making up fables and proverbs shouldn't be looked on as solely the province of artists or young people. As adults we can all stand to play a bit with language, to step out of our usual modes of functioning, and let ourselves draw and write for the pleasure these activities can provide for us and our friends.

Further Reading

Allen, W. *Without Feathers*. New York: Random House, 1972.

Anaya, R. *Bless Me, Ultima*. New York: Warner Books, 1994.

Brown, C. *Manchild in the Promised Land*. New York: Penguin Books, 1965.

Chevigny, B. G. (ed.). *Doing Time: Twenty-Five Years of Prison Writing*. New York: Arcade Publishing, 1999.

Cofer, J. O. *Silent Dancing: A Partial Remembrance of a Puerto Rican Childhood*. Houston: Arte Publico Press, 1990.

Douglass, F. *The Life and Times of Frederick Douglass*. New York: Collier Books, 1962.

Grimes, N. *Jazmin's Notebook*. New York: Puffin Books, 1998.

Harper, M. S., and Walton, A. (eds.). *Every Shut Eye Ain't Asleep: An Anthology of Poetry by African Americans Since 1945*. New York: Little, Brown, 1994.

Harrison, D. *Wild Country: Outdoor Poems for Young People*. Honesdale, Pa.: Boyds Mills Press, 1999.

Heng, L., and Shapiro, J. *Son of the Revolution*. New York: Knopf, 1983.

Hirsch, J.S.H. *The Miraculous Journey of Ruben Carter*. Boston: Houghton Mifflin, 2000.

Holliday, L. (ed.). *Dreaming in Color, Living in Black and White: Our Own Stories of Growing Up Black in America*. New York: Pocket Books, 2000.

Hong Kingston, M. *Woman Warrior*. New York: Knopf, 1990.

Jiménez, F. *The Circuit: Stories from the Life of a Migrant Child*. Albuquerque: University of New Mexico Press, 1997.

Jiménez, F. *Breaking Through: Sequel to* The Circuit. Boston: Houghton Mifflin, 2001.

Jordan, J. *Soldier: A Poet's Childhood*. New York: Basic Civitas Books, 2000.

Jordan, V. E., Jr., with Gordon-Reed, A. *Vernon Can Read: A Memoir*. Washington, D.C.: Public Affairs Press, 2000.

Kazin, A. *A Walker in the City*. New York: Grove Press, 1951.

Lee, H. (ed.). *The Secret Self 1: Short Stories by Women*. London: Everyman, 1985.

Mazer, A. (ed.). *Going Where I'm Coming From: Memoirs of American Youth, A Multicultural Anthology*. New York: Persea Books, 1995.

McCloud, S. *Understanding Comics: The Invisible Art*. New York: HarperCollins, 1993.

McCurdy, M. (ed.). *Escape from Slavery: The Boyhood of Frederick Douglass in His Own Words*. New York: Knopf, 1994.

Ohanian, S. *Ask Ms. Class*. Yarmouth, Me.: Stenhouse Publishers, 1995.

Paulsen, G. *The Winter Room*. New York: Orchard Books, 1989.

Paulsen, G. *Nightjohn*. New York: Bantam Books, 1993.

Poitier, S. *The Measure of a Man: A Spiritual Autobiography*. New York: Harper-Collins, 2001.

Polacco, P. *Thank You Mr. Falker*. New York: Philomel Books, 1998.

Rochelle, B. *Words with Wings: A Treasury of African-American Poetry and Art*. New York: HarperCollins, 2001.

Rodriguez, L. J. *Always Running: La Vida Loca, Gang Days in L.A.* New York: Touchstone, 1994.

Rodriguez, L. J. *It Doesn't Have to Be This Way: A Barrio Story*. San Francisco: Children's Book Press. 1999.

Rodriguez, R. *Hunger of Memory: The Education of Richard Rodriguez*. New York: Bantam Books, 1982.

Rose, M. *Lives on the Boundary: A Moving Account of the Struggles and Achievements of America's Educational Underclass*. New York: Penguin Books, 1980.

Saldana, R., Jr. *The Jumping Tree, a Novel*. New York: Delacorte Press, 2001.

Salisbury, G. *Blue Skin of the Seas*. New York: Dell, 1992.

Schwartz, M. *Luis Rodriguez: Writer, Community Leader, Political Activist*. Austin, Tex.: Steck-Vaughn, 1997.

Spinelli, J. *Maniac Magee*. New York: Little, Brown, 1990.

Wright, R. *Black Boy: A Record of Childhood and Youth*. New York: Harper-Collins, 1937.

X, Malcolm, and Haley, A. *The Autobiography of Malcolm X*. New York: Random House, 1964.

About the Editors

Audrey Fielding is a consultant with the Strategic Literacy Initiative of WestEd and the Bay Area Writing Project. She has been involved in English language arts instruction as a teacher, resource teacher, and bilingual teacher at the middle and high school levels in Costa Rica and the San Francisco Bay Area for a number of years. For the past ten years, she has worked as a literacy coach with teachers in Northern California, El Salvador, and Namibia. Her writing has appeared in National and Bay Area Writing Project publications, the National and Northern California Peace Corps Newsletters, and *Sistersong: Women Across Cultures*, a literary journal. She has a master's degree in secondary education from San Francisco State University and is a graduate of the Master of Arts in Writing Program at the University of San Francisco.

Ruth Schoenbach is codirector of the Strategic Literacy Initiative at WestEd. She has coauthored *Reading for Understanding: A Guide to Improving Reading in Middle and High School Classrooms* (Jossey-Bass, 1999) and a number of articles, including "Apprenticing Adolescent Readers to Academic Literacy" (*Harvard Educational Review*, Spring 2001). From 1988 to 1996, she directed the Humanities Education, Research, and Language Development Project in the San

Francisco Unified School District, where she had worked previously as a classroom teacher and curriculum developer. She has a master's degree from the Harvard Graduate School of Education in teaching, curriculum, and learning environments.

About the Sponsor

WestEd

WestEd is a nonprofit research, development, and service agency that works with education and other communities to promote excellence, achieve equity, and improve learning for children, youth, and adults. The agency collaborates with a variety of individuals and institutions to accomplish a range of objectives, including helping children enter school healthy and eager to learn; tailoring effective assessment strategies for states and districts; helping to bring about successful schoolwide change; enhancing teachers' career-long professional development; and finding ways for community-based groups to collaborate and solve problems. One of the nation's Regional Educational Laboratories, WestEd serves Arizona, California, Nevada, and Utah. Its work also extends throughout the rest of the country—with projects in forty-four states—and internationally.

For more information, visit www.wested.org.

Strategic Literacy Initiative

The Strategic Literacy Initiative (SLI) at WestEd is a professional development and research program focusing on improving adolescent literacy as a means to increasing the academic access, engagement, and achievement of diverse urban middle school and high school students. SLI has documented gains in students' reading comprehension, with students who are second-language learners and those who score in the bottom two quartiles on standardized tests of reading comprehension showing the greatest gains.[1]

The program's centerpiece is an inquiry-based professional development program based on the Reading Apprenticeship™ framework described in SLI's book *Reading for Understanding: A Guide to Improving Reading in Middle and High School Classrooms*, by Ruth Schoenbach, Cynthia Greenleaf, Christine Cziko, and Lori Hurwitz (Jossey-Bass, 1999). This instructional framework emphasizes:

- Making the teacher's discipline-based reading processes and knowledge visible to students

- Making students' reading processes, motivations, strategies, knowledge, and understandings visible to the teacher and to one another

- Helping students gain and learn to use insight into their own reading processes

- Helping students develop a repertoire of problem-solving strategies for overcoming obstacles and deepening their comprehension of texts from various academic disciplines

The SLI conducts professional development programs for cross-school networks of interdisciplinary teams of middle and high school teachers in the San Francisco Bay Area. In addition, it offers National Institutes on Reading Apprenticeship™ nationwide for educators who are responsible for teacher professional development.

For more information on SLI's research, tools, and programs, see www.wested.org/stratlit.

The SLI is supported in part by grants from the following foundations: the Carnegie Foundation, the William and Flora Hewlett

Foundation, the Walter S. Johnson Foundation, and the Stuart Foundations.

This book project in particular was produced with generous support from the Stupski Family Foundation.

Note

1. C. Greenleaf, R. Schoenbach, C. Cziko, and F. Mueller, "Apprenticing Adolescent Readers to Academic Literacy," *Harvard Educational Review* (Spring 2001): 79–129.

Sources and Permissions

CHAPTER FIVE

"My Back Pages" by Greg Sarris, from *The Most Wonderful Books: Writers on Discovering the Pleasures of Reading*, edited by Michael Dorris and Emile Buchwald. (Minneapolis, Minn.: Milkweed Editions, 1997), pp. 223–224. Reprinted with permission from Frederick Hill Bonnie Nadell Inc.

CHAPTER SIX

"Seis," from *Bless Me, Ultima* by Rudolfo A. Anaya. (Upper Saddle River, N.J.: Prentice Hall, K–12 Edition, Reprint May 1995). Copyright © 1974 by Rudolfo Anaya. Published in hardcover and mass paperback by Warner Books, Inc., 1994; originally published by TQS Publications. Reprinted by permission of Susan Bergholz Literary Services, New York. All rights reserved.

CHAPTER SEVEN

"Discovering Books," from Chapter XIII from *Black Boy: A Record of Childhood and Youth* by Richard Wright. (New York: Harper-Collins Publishers, 1969), pp. 214–222. Copyright © 1937, 1942, 1944, 1945 by Richard Wright. Copyright renewed 1973 by Ellen Wright. Reprinted by permission of HarperCollins Publishers Inc.

CHAPTER EIGHT

"The Gift of Reading," from *Better Than Life* by Daniel Pennac, translated by David Homel. (Portland, Me.: Stenhouse Publishers, 1999). Copyright © 1992 Editions Gallimard. Used by permission of Editions Gallimard.

CHAPTER NINE

"Coming into Language," from *Doing Time: Twenty-Five Years of Prison Writing* by Jimmy Santiago Baca. Edited by Bell Gale Chevigny. (New York: Arcade Publishing Inc., 1999), pp. 100–106. Copyright © 1999 by PEN American Center. Used by permission of Jimmy Santiago Baca.

CHAPTER TEN

"Silence," from *Woman Warrior* by Maxine Hong Kingston. (New York: Alfred A. Knopf, 1990), pp. 163–169. Copyright 1975, 1976 by Maxine Hong Kingston. Used by permission of Alfred A. Knopf, a division of Random House, Inc.

CHAPTER ELEVEN

"Aria: A Memoir of a Bilingual Childhood," from *Hunger of Memory: The Education of Richard Rodriguez* by Richard Rodriguez. (New York: Bantam Books, Reissue Edition, 1983). Copyright © 1982 by Richard Rodriguez. Reprinted by permission of David R. Godine, Publisher, Inc.

CHAPTER TWELVE

"Reading Has Always Been My Home," from *How Reading Changed My Life* by Anna Quindlen. (New York: Ballantine Books, 1998). Copyright © 1998 by Anna Quindlen. Used by permission of Ballantine Books, a division of Random House, Inc.

CHAPTER THIRTEEN

"Brownsville Schooldays," from *A Walker in the City* by Alfred Kazin. (First Grove Press Edition, 1958, eighth printing), pp. 17–24. Copyright © 1951 and renewed 1979 by Alfred Kazin. Reprinted by permission of Harcourt, Inc.

CHAPTER FOURTEEN

"Gary Lee," from *Speaking of Reading*, edited by Nadine Rosenthal. (Portsmouth, N.H.: Heinemann, 1995), pp. 145–148. Copyright © 1995 by Nadine Rosenthal. Reprinted by permission of Nadine Rosenthal.

CHAPTER FIFTEEN

"Two Ways to Be a Warrior," from *Luis Rodriguez: Writer, Community Leader, Political Activist* by Michael Schwartz. (Austin, Tex.: Steck-Vaughn Company, 1997), pp. 5–11. Copyright © 1997 Steck-Vaughn Company. All rights reserved. Permission granted by arrangement with Steck-Vaughn Company.

CHAPTER SIXTEEN
Excerpt from "The Poets in the Kitchen," from *Reena and Other Stories* by Paule Marshall. (New York: Feminist Press, 1983), pp. 9–11. Copyright © 1983 by Paule Marshall. Used by permission of the Feminist Press at the City University of New York, www.feministpress.org.

CHAPTER SEVENTEEN
"Libraries and the Attack on Illiteracy" by Timothy S. Healy, S.J. Used by permission of the Estate of Timothy S. Healy, S.J., and the New York Province of the Society of Jesus.

CHAPTER EIGHTEEN
"Learning to Read," from *The Autobiography of Malcolm X* by Malcolm X and Alex Haley. (New York: Random House, 1989). Copyright © 1964 by Alex Haley and Malcolm X. Copyright © 1965 by Alex Haley and Betty Shabazz. Used by permission of Random House, Inc.

CHAPTER NINETEEN
"In Conversation with Ernest J. Gaines" by Adrianne Bee. From *San Francisco State University Magazine* (Fall 2000, Vol. 1, No. 1), pp. 24, 26–27. Used by permission of Adrianne Bee and *San Francisco State University Magazine*.

CHAPTER TWENTY
"Learning to Read" by Frances E. W. Harper. 19CWWW Etext Library. http://www.unl.edu/legacy/19cwww/books/elibe/harper/harchloe/htm.

CHAPTER TWENTY-ONE
"Precious Words" by Emily Dickinson. Reprinted by permission of the publishers and the Trustees of Amherst College from *The Poems of Emily Dickinson*, edited by Thomas H. Johnson. (Cambridge, Mass.: Belknap Press of Harvard University Press, 1976), p. 1587. Copyright © 1951, 1955, 1979 by the President and Fellows of Harvard College.

CHAPTER TWENTY-TWO
"Learning to Read and Write" by Frederick Douglass, from *Frederick Douglass: Autobiographies: Narrative of the Life of Frederick Douglass, an American Slave*. (New York: The Library of America, 1994), pp. 39–45. Copyright © 1994 by Literary Classics of the United States, Inc.

CHAPTER TWENTY-THREE
"India's Literary Miracle." The editors have made diligent efforts to locate the source of this selection and to obtain permission to reprint it but have been unsuccessful.

CHAPTER TWENTY-FOUR
"Interrogation," from *Son of the Revolution* by Liang Heng and Judith Shapiro. (New York: Alfred A. Knopf, 1983), pp. 201–208. Copyright © 1983 by Liang Heng and Judith Shapiro. Used by permission of Alfred A. Knopf, a division of Random House, Inc.

CHAPTER TWENTY-FIVE
"Reign of the Reader" by M. Freeman. From *Reading Today*, 19(3). (Newark, Del.: International Reading Association, Dec. 2001/Jan. 2002), p. 30. Reprinted with permission of the International Reading Association. All rights reserved.

CHAPTER TWENTY-SIX
"Gerald Eisman," from *Speaking of Reading*, edited by Nadine Rosenthal. (Portsmouth, N.H.: Heinemann, 1995), pp. 163–165. Copyright © 1995 by Nadine Rosenthal. Reprinted by permission of Nadine Rosenthal.

CHAPTER TWENTY-SEVEN
"The Voice You Hear When You Read Silently," from *New and Selected Poems* by Thomas Lux. (Boston: Houghton Mifflin Company, 1997.) Copyright © 1997 by Thomas Lux. Reprinted by permission of Houghton Mifflin Company. All rights reserved. Previously published in *The New Yorker*.

CHAPTER THIRTY-FOUR
"Three Wise Guys: *Un Cuento de Navidad*/A Christmas Story" by Sandra Cisneros. From *Mexican American Literature*, edited by Charles Tatum. (Florida: Harcourt Brace Jovanovich, 1990), pp. 331–337. Copyright © 1990 by Sandra Cisneros. First published by *VISTA Magazine*, December 23, 1990. Reprinted by permission of Susan Bergholz Literary Services, New York. All rights reserved.

CHAPTER THIRTY-FIVE
"The New Case for Latin" by Mike Eskenazi. *Time Magazine* (Dec. 11, 2000). Copyright © 2000 TIME Inc., reprinted by permission.

CHAPTER THIRTY-SIX
"No Words," from *Wild Country: Outdoor Poems for Young People* by David Harrison. (Honesdale, Pa.: Boyds Mills Press, Inc., 1999.) Text copyright © 1999 by David Harrison. Reprinted by permission.

CHAPTER THIRTY-SEVEN
"Teaching People to Hate Literature" by Matthew S., Lexington, Mass. (http://TeenInk.com/Past/1991/1366.html). Copyright © 2000 by TeenInk, The 21st Century and The Young Authors Foundation, Inc. Reprinted with permission from TeenInk and The Young Authors Foundation. All rights reserved.

CHAPTER THIRTY-EIGHT
"Team Xerox" by Chris Taylor. *Time Magazine* (Nov. 4, 2000). Copyright © 2000 TIME Inc., reprinted by permission.

CHAPTER THIRTY-NINE
"Private Reading," from *A History of Reading* by Alberto Manguel. (New York: Viking Penguin, 1996), pp. 150–153. Copyright © 1996 by Alberto Manguel. Used by permission of Penguin, a division of Penguin Putnam Inc.

CHAPTER FORTY
"Susan Schulter," from *Speaking of Reading*, edited by Nadine Rosenthal. (Portsmouth, N.H.: Heinemann, 1995), pp. 14–17. Copyright

CHAPTER FORTY-ONE

CHAPTER FORTY-TWO

CHAPTER FORTY-THREE

CHAPTER FORTY-FOUR

CHAPTER FORTY-FIVE

CHAPTER FORTY-SIX

Reading for Understanding: A Guide to Improving Reading in Middle and High School Classrooms

Ruth Schoenbach, Cynthia Greenleaf,
Christine Cziko, and Lori Hurwitz
Copublished with WestEd
Paperback, December 1999, 240 pp., 8-1/2 × 11,
$21.00, ISBN 0-7879-5045-9

This book introduces the nationally recognized Reading Apprenticeship™ instructional framework, a research-based model with a proven record of success in increasing the engagement and achievement of adolescent readers, including many considered "struggling" or disengaged students. Filled with vivid classroom lessons and exercises, the book shows teachers how to "apprentice" students to reading in the disciplines, an approach that demystifies the reading process for students so they can acquire the necessary motivational, cognitive, and knowledge-building strategies for comprehending diverse and challenging types of texts. The book also presents a detailed description of the pilot "Academic Literacy" curriculum, a year-long course in which a group of urban ninth-grade students made an average of two years' gain in reading comprehension. In addition, it shows how Reading Apprenticeship™ strategies can be embedded in science, math, English, and social studies classrooms, thus serving as a useful guide for teachers working across the curricula in grades 6–12.

Building Academic Literacy: Lessons from Reading Apprenticeship Classrooms, Grades 6–12

Audrey Fielding, Ruth Schoenbach,
and Marean Jordan, Editors
Copublished with WestEd
Paperback, April 2003, 192 pp., 6 × 9, $18.00,
ISBN 0-7879-6556-1

Featuring pieces by five practicing teachers, this book shows how the Reading Apprenticeship™ instructional framework can be adapted to diverse classrooms and teaching styles. Filled with insights and guidance on strengthening adolescent literacy, the book includes instructional tips, lesson plans, and classroom exercises for enabling students to become independent, strategic, and competent readers, serving as a vital resource for English/language arts teachers in grades 6–12. The book also includes extensive resource tools for implementing Academic Literacy course units, as well as examples of classroom practices using selections from *Building Academic Literacy: An Anthology for Reading Apprenticeship* (Fielding and Schoenbach, 0-7879-6555-3), making this an invaluable teacher companion to the related student reader.

[Prices subject to change]